A New Breed: Satellite Terrorism In America

Dr. John Hall

Strategic Book Publishing
New York, NewYork

Strategic Book Publishing
An imprint of Writers Literary & Publishing Services, Inc.
845 Third Avenue, 6th Floor – 6016
New York, NY 10022
http://www.strategicbookpublishing.com

ISBN: 978-1-60693-944-4, 1-60693-944-0

Printed in the United States of America

"May God Have Mercy Upon My Enemies, Because I Won't . . . "
—General George Patton, Jr.

Dedication

For "M", whom so many have sacrificed to help you; may God grant you the strength to help yourself.

Acknowledgements

This book would have never come to fruition without the assistance of many people...Super Nurse Kathy, Priscilla, Jana and Rachel, for believing in me and assisting me in this endeavor even when it meant endangering their lives.

Special "thanks" to Dr. David Kaiser, my colleague and partner, for putting up with all the weird things that happened to us while trying to get this book written and published.

Alice Herrera-Rutkowsky, my virtual assistant at Wings Typing and Notary Service. She was harder on my spelling and grammar than any editor I could possibly find!

Cherie McCarter, for her invaluable stamina while doing much of the research for this book and for her continued support in my second one.

As for all the TI's out there, there will be an end to this. Remember that knowledge is power and what you understand cannot hurt you!

Table of Contents

Preface

While you are having sex, unless you are an exhibitionist, you probably close the door to the bedroom. You probably make sure the blinds or shutters are closed just in case a nosey neighbor with a telescope may be watching. Even worse, there may be voyeurs with cameras who place themselves at your windows hoping to put you and your significant other on the Web.

Let's face it, amateur and voyeur pornography is booming with the advent of the Internet and relative anonymity of its producers and customers. Now, imagine they do not need cameras to see inside your bedroom, hear your phone calls, hear your very thoughts and control your moods and actions. This technology would allow a group of criminals to break into your home, when they know you're away and neighbors aren't watching. They spend days successfully hiding high-definition cameras and microphones in walls, appliances, and ceilings. Bingo! Your sex life is now open to viewing on a plethora of domestic and foreign sex Web sites unknown to you of course... Members only, please!

Imagine no further, this technology does exist. It's called satellite surveillance; a weapon meant for government use that's being hacked into by criminals for very sinister purposes. Its classified technology that the Government cannot admit exists, regardless of the lack of safeguards keeping the system from being hacked into. They know the cat is out of the bag and won't do anything about it! Everyone is familiar with the pandemonium the government had to deal with involving the Patriot Act, FBI or NSA phone taps and loss of privacy. The ACLU has given them hell over the basics. In today's climate, the government is not going to admit losing control of a satellite surveillance

7

system capable of seeing you indoors, controlling your thoughts, hearing your thoughts, and attacking you to keep you in line.

The book you're about to read is an account of this technology gone way astray. I've put up with it for years, as have others. It may read like fiction...it's not. Thousands of people are being targeted by criminals accessing this satellite surveillance system. In my case, at least, I know who they are! The names have been changed to protect the guilty, pending further investigation and litigation. Big Brother is definitely watching ...but he may be one of your neighbors, not the government.

Chapter 1

Background

Before starting medical school in Ft. Worth, Texas I worked as an operating room technician in San Antonio, my hometown, and now my permanent residence. I attended several universities eventually earning a Bachelor of Science degree in Biology from the University of Texas at San Antonio, with a minor in Philosophy and Theology. I made some close friends in college, and partied when I could and worked when I should.

After losing my girlfriend in a drunken automobile wreck on the Texas coast, my life began to change. She had gone to the beach on Spring Break with a girlfriend who had gotten drunk and driven them at high speed into a telephone pole. Merry was killed instantly. I found out one month later after going to her parents' house wondering why I hadn't heard from her.

We had argued about her going on this trip. The meeting was dramatic for her mother and me. The whole thing was brought back to the forefront of her mother's mind by my visit and I came away depressed and enraged at myself for not checking into what happened to her sooner. My life changed drastically after that day.

I submerged myself in school and work, cutting back on the partying in an attempt to keep a GPA good enough to enter medical school. I was working part-time at an ambulatory surgical center as an anesthesia technician. The center was partially owned by a group of physicians, one of whom was Dr. Harry Shelby, MD. Shelby, an ear nose and throat surgeon, did the bulk of the cases there. Mostly children getting ear tubes, tonsillectomies, and nasal endoscopies. He had long since traded doing the more difficult neck and cancer type surgeries for the ambulatory easy-life.

Young, healthy patients went home at the end of the day and were taken care of in lucrative bulk. Those surgeries made Shelby a lot of money without a lot of patient follow-up, hospital admissions or hospital calls. I guess he figured he had paid his dues with the long-term patients and left the more serious surgeries to his partners.

Dr. Cohen is a gregarious character, silver haired and red-cheeked, with a somewhat volatile temperament. He tries to personify the "good ole Texas boy" character. He is a consummate hunter and fisherman, preferring a Ford F-250 to a Mercedes to pull off his "good ole boy" characterization. When we first met, he was a lot of fun to be around. We worked hard and we played even harder. However, Dr. Cohen had a dark side; he was a heavy drinker. His favorites are black label Jack Daniels, vodka and grapefruit and Franzia wine by the box. Quite the womanizer, he has a wife and two sons, a long-time girlfriend and prostitutes on every hunting and fishing trip too numerous to mention here. He's a "guy's guy" if you know what I mean. He's fun to be around, but you wouldn't want to be married to him and certainly wouldn't want him married to your sister! Little did I know in 1987 that befriending him would ruin my life and the life of my fiancée years later.

I entered medical school at the University of North Texas Health Science Center in Ft. Worth in 1988. I visited San Antonio quite often the first two years, working part-time during the summer and courting my wife-to-be, Kathy. We eventually married and I became husband and instant father to two very rambunctious boys from her previous marriage. As with most medical students, I was absorbed by my curricular demands and paid little attention to the family. By the time I finished medical school I received my medical degree and a divorce simultaneously. Very few marriages survive the grueling schedule and sacrifices that medical school imposes on you. Mine was no different.

Content to be single until I at least started residency, I screwed anything with a vagina in the greater Dallas/Ft. Worth area while Kathy took her kids back to San Antonio. As a graduating medical student, I looked into various residency programs. I entered my name into a "match system" which matches interviewees with specific training programs across the U.S. As a prospect, I ranked the programs I wanted to attend and the programs ranked me on desired residency program.

Somewhere in a dark basement a state-of-the-art computer program matched me up with a residency program after publishing my results on the back page of a USA Today newspaper. It appears that my destiny was already in place. When match day finally came I knew the location of my future home.

Fortunately two of my closest friends and I were destined for the State of Ohio. I rode a motorcycle to medical school every day wearing only T-shirts and cut-off denim shorts...come rain or shine! Living in Texas gets one accustomed to thinking "we don't need a coat"!

In 1992 Michael Lissner, Ken Stephens and I left for the Great White North. We started our orthopedic, neurology and anesthesia residencies respectfully. Following completion of our training we went our separate ways, yet we have remained life-long friends. Scattered among the grueling work days with little pay, the three of us managed to get a lot of scuba diving done in Cozumel, Mexico...our home away from home.

Upon finishing residency, Mike moved back to Colorado, Glen stayed in Cleveland and I returned to San Antonio. We've stayed in touch over the years, but I have never confided in them what I found lurking in San Antonio upon my return home. Mike was finally getting married, Glen was finally getting divorced and I decided my troubles were just that...my troubles.

Chapter 2

Home, Sweet Home?

In 1996 I returned to San Antonio, Texas to start my medical practice. After four years of residency I was finally an Anesthesiologist. Four years earlier I couldn't spell "anesthesiologist" and now I was one of those! In school and residency they teach you medicine but they don't really teach you the business end of it. Trial and error ensued. I began to figure out how to set up a practice, get malpractice insurance, attract patients and referrals, get privileges at hospitals, get my billing done and still make time for some semblance of a life. Things went relatively smoothly at first. I got an apartment with a garage to house my Harley Davidson and Isuzu Amigo, earned my board certification and my practice got off to a pretty good start.

Anesthesiology groups that had refused me straight out of residency were now asking me to join them. Screw them, I thought! They weren't there for me when I needed them, so why join them now? Dr. Harry Shelby re-surfaced in my life and asked me to do his anesthesia on Wednesday and Friday mornings. I accepted. Life didn't look too bad after all.

Mary had moved down from Youngstown, Ohio to San Antonio with me after residency. She was a petite, strawberry blonde girl of Italian descent. Very well educated, she had earned her Master's degree in Dietary Science at Westminster College. She was continually pursuing higher education; she said it was, "to compete with me having earned a medical degree." I never could convince her that I loved her, not the initials behind her name! She came from a strict Church of Christ upbringing and living together was out of the question, so I "put her up" in a nearby apartment complex. I was divorced, and that was unacceptable in their religion. Her parents were less than thrilled about her seeing me and were quite vocal about that. Although semi-alienated from her family she remained with me in San Antonio. She looked for gainful employment and was immediately offered the position of Chief Dietician at the Baptist Hospital.

Mary carried some psychological baggage from her past that resurfaced once she moved to San Antonio--and for good reason! At sixteen she was savagely beaten, raped and left on a deserted country road outside Youngstown, Ohio. Her parents blamed her, as she had crept out of the house to meet an eighteen year old boy they knew to be trouble. He beat her, raped her, and tried to get his friends to rape her as well. Her parents were in fear of embarrassment if it came out that she had crept out of the house to meet him. There were no charges filed. Date rape wasn't the crime then as it is now. He got away with the rape and she became anorexic and ended up with a hospital stay. Her battle with anorexia prompted her interest in Dietetics.

Not long after moving to San Antonio her personality began to change. She became highly temperamental and her diet started to relapse back into her eating disorder as an anorexic. Dry salads, black coffee and purging became the daily norm. We'd go to a restaurant, I'd have a steak, and she would order water and a dry salad.

Her apartment started getting broken into and her things rifled through, but nothing ever actually stolen. On several occasions I found her too tired to even leave the apartment. At the time I wasn't thinking that she was being drugged, but looking back now, I'm not so sure that wasn't the case. Nonetheless, we both thought it best for her to return to Ohio. As the future would bear out, she went back to Ohio, married and had a child and is doing great at the present time. Her future wouldn't have been as bright had she stayed in San Antonio, a city plagued by a new breed of sex offenders.

Chapter 3

The Nuts And Bolts

In 1998, we saw the release of the movie, "Enemy of the State" starring Will Smith as the main character. In the movie he's trying his best to evade rogue NSA agents tracking his every movement with satellite surveillance and high definition cameras on helicopters and in buildings. It may have seemed far-fetched at the time, but the technology was already in existence then and has surpassed even the dreams of most science fiction writers. Anyone can hide radio-frequency cameras in your house and sit outside to monitor and record your actions. That's old technology that has been in existence a long time, evidenced by tanning salon operators selling voyeur pornography to Web sites. I'm not focusing on that. Satellite surveillance has taken invasion of privacy to an all new high. The current satellite surveillance systems used by the government, and those illegally accessing it, can see you indoors and out, alter your moods, hear your thoughts, attack you with weaponry and access your financial accounts. It's no longer science fiction when it's really happening to thousands of people across the United States and uncounted numbers worldwide. It's a psychiatrist's dream come true: thousands of people with a real problem, wrongfully diagnosed and treated with medicines and therapy that work minimally in people with psychiatric problems. People hearing voices aren't always delusional!

Sometimes these voices are being generated by a criminal in front of a computer wearing a headset and trying his best to drive you crazy. John Fleming touched on the problem in 1996 when he wrote "The Shocking Menace of Satellite Surveillance." It can be reviewed on a multitude of Web sites and is probably worthwhile for you to Google if you're reading this book. In 1996 it was probably viewed by most as fantasy; however, many people are taking a closer look now. His description of satellite imagery and weaponry is fairly complete. Everyone has been on Google maps and seen the advancements in basic satellite imaging. One is able to see their street, their rooftop and businesses nearby. The technology is leaps and bounds above what you're able to see there. CIA and NSA satellite systems cannot only read the writing on a penny outside, but can see you indoors (through your walls) as well. That is, unless you're living with Osama Bin Laden three hundred feet beneath a rock mountain! You may be safe then! An array of imaging modalities that are used include thermal infrared, basic camera imaging, and X-ray. Obviously basic imaging and infrared can detect you clearly if you're outside or in front of an open window. But indoors you ask? X-ray. Actually, X-ray and thermal imaging can both make you visible indoors. What they're seeing is an X-ray image very similar to what you might see in a medical X-ray, but in real time. Thermal images are similar in quality to X-ray images and in much better contrast than the blue, red and orange pictures seen in movies like "Predator." All in all the imaging part of satellite surveillance is probably the easiest part to grasp. The take home message is if you're being targeted, they know where you are inside your house and probably where your neighbors are as well. The imaging alone allows for easy breaking and entering since the criminals will know when you're not home and your neighbors aren't watching.

Auditory harassment is another mainstay of the criminal element using satellite surveillance. If a government agency is watching you they're probably not going to verbally abuse you while attacking you for years at a time. They'll watch you, listen, attack if needed and move on if you're of no interest. Not so with criminals using the system. Their goal is to drive you crazy or at best make you look crazy by auditory harassing you. This is accomplished through what is known as non-auditory hearing or microwave hearing, in addition to ultra low frequency broadcasting. In simplest terms, a frequency can be found where a targeted individual can be transmitted a conversation that no one else around them can hear. The implications of this shouldn't need further mention. These ultra-low frequency broadcasts are voices that are heard in vibrations around the targeted individual. For example, voices that sound like people talking outside your window or conversations coming through the vibrations in a bathroom ventilator fan. They are being transmitted and intended for the targeted individual to hear and not others around them.

Microwave hearing differs from ULF broadcasting very uniquely. The NSA, CIA, Army, and Defense Advanced Research Projects Agency (DARPA)-funded agencies have spent millions researching and perfecting this technology. It works by using direct microwave transmitted sound to the cochlear microphone system of the ear. This is actually old technology, perfected for current and future use. The science behind it can be read about in the Army's "Addendum to the Nonlethal Technologies" (NGIC-1147-101-98). Essentially, microwave hearing amounts to hearing voices in your head that aren't your own. The early value of this technology was to help the deaf be able to hear; however, once picked up by the government it found other uses. As you're reading this book you're hearing your own voice in your head. Now, imagine someone can mimic your voice and place what sounds like your thoughts in your head. Voila'! You have true mind control.

As a matter of fact in the above-mentioned Army document it states; "It may be useful to provide a disruptive condition to a person not aware of this technology. Not only might it be disruptive to the sense of hearing, it could be psychologically-devastating if one suddenly heard voices within one's head." The document goes on to mention that recorders placed next to the targeted individuals head cannot record the transmitted voices they're being made to hear.

Cheryl Weinberger, a journalist, in her article in the Washington Post interviewed and wrote of people nationwide who are under the assumption that they are under satellite surveillance. In her report she interviewed an engineering student in San Antonio, Texas. He actually had been an anesthesiology resident just about to complete his residency when he started hearing voices in his head and around him that no one else could hear. He was unable to get licensed as a physician due to psychiatric treatment for his "auditory delusions" and changed careers to engineering. After psychiatric treatment he continued hearing the voices, thus causing him and his wife to divorce.

He noted that the voices were not just in his head, but also sounded like neighbors conversing outside his window; is this sounding familiar? The psychiatrist that treated him never bothered asking him what the voices were saying. He was left hearing the criminals harassing him claiming; "We'll never leave you alone!" If this sounds like science fiction so far...it's not, and it gets worse...much worse.

Chapter 4

The Spooky Stuff

If advanced satellite imaging isn't scary enough, it gets worse. If you've ever been to a neurologist or had an anesthetic for surgery, you've probably had an EEG or spectral analysis of your EEG called BIS. BIS was invented so the anesthesiologist can determine awareness, or lack of, while you're asleep for surgery. After several horror stories about people waking up during surgery, BIS became pretty standard monitoring in operating rooms.

EEG monitoring gives you a graph of the electrical activity of the brain broken down into frequency and waveforms. Basically each waveform represents a different functional state of the brain. This isn't a medical textbook, but understanding the basic technology is important in understanding the more advanced technology that we're up against. EEG tracing shows the brain in its state of wakefulness or sleep by demonstrating alpha, beta, theta or delta waves. Alpha and beta waves are present when you're awake. Delta waves occur during deep sleep. The theta waves occur during REM sleep or dream sleep. During REM sleep the reading of your state of consciousness through EEG is primo to perpetrators of satellite voyeurism. There are also a myriad of measurements called evoked potentials. With electrodes placed on the skull, specific brain electrical activity can be measured graphically when you feel, hear, see or smell something. These evoked potential monitors are commonly used in brain and spinal surgery to make sure neural pathways remain normal during surgery. Now you're current on brain monitoring as was the state of the art up to about 1950! Defense Advanced Research Projects Agency (DARPA) has taken brain monitoring technology quite a bit further than the antiquated monitoring we're still using today in medicine. Every time you have a thought electrical and biochemical changes occur in your brain. Advanced technology has allowed these changes to be monitored, measured and recorded. The two latest advances include surface EEG processing and functional MRI or fMRI. Functional MRI, the less classified of the two, displays biochemical changes in the brain during thought and is in current use for lie detection.

Every thought you hear, emotion you feel or any lie you tell will light up different areas of the brain allowing those monitoring you to assess your emotional state and honesty. Researchers claim the fMRI is still being investigated as to its safety in human use. The ACLU is worried about it supposedly already being put to use in surveillance satellite systems. Jonathan Moreno touched on this in his book "Mind Wars: Brain Research and National Defense." Functional MRI is not being used in legitimate medical practice. It is strictly an intelligence tool at this point. So, don't go asking your physician to schedule you for an fMRI...he won't know what you're talking about.

Surface EEG processing is more troublesome and much more secretive. Every time you have a thought a ripple of electrical activity skips across the surface of the brain. This electrical activity can be picked up much the same way the basic EEG monitors record gross electrical activity at the neurologist's office. The fundamental difference between basic EEG monitoring and EEG processing is the software that exists which converts electrical impulses right back into language. So, essentially, you have a thought that generates surface brain electrical activity that gets received and converted back into your voice for a monitor to hear with little or no delay. Remember earlier in the book I mentioned, as a reader, you can hear your voice in your head as you read and comprehend the words...so can they! Mind reading has finally come of age without the use of tarot cards or a crystal ball thanks to government research. Surface EEG processing has allowed brain fingerprinting to be accomplished, as every individual has a different surface EEG pattern not unlike different fingerprints on the hand. The installation of this technology on satellite systems allows not only tracking of an individual by body and facial image recollection, but by an individual's brain fingerprint. Once you're targeted and in the system you can be found anywhere and picked out of a crowd of thousands to be observed and listened to. In a world of dwindling privacy due to phone taps, hidden cameras and microphones, the government has finally found a way to get into the last bastion of privacy...your mind.

As I mentioned earlier, your brain responds electrically every time you feel, see, smell, or hear. One can measure these responses with monitors that are used routinely in surgical and medical settings. So can they, but with one major difference. Medical monitoring allows us to see a bunch of squiggly lines alluding to the patient's feeling, hearing or smelling something. Surface EEG monitoring in satellite surveillance use allows monitors to hear and see what you actually are hearing and seeing. In effect, your brain, after being targeted, becomes the camera and the microphone. So, now one can see how easily someone is watched, tracked, harassed and controlled via satellite. If you're a terrorist plotting against the United States I guess a good argument can be made for you deserving it. Unfortunately, non-government criminals are also hacking into the system to commit crimes against innocent individuals like you and me.

For the scientifically inclined, a list of mind control symptoms, complete with references to the studies behind them, can be viewed at http://www.mindjustice.org/symptoms.html. Another group that has compiled a lot of information on the subject is Freedom from Covert Harassment and Surveillance. Their Website is http://www.freedomfchs.com. Don't think for a minute that you have to be a head of state or CEO of some large corporation to be a victim. That is the biggest misconception! The criminals, not the government using this system are interested in wholesale torture, sexual assault and stealing money. People being harassed always think, "Why would the government want to mess with me...I'm nobody. Exactly. The government probably wouldn't want to mess with you; there's no need.

The technology has been around for quite a few years with no need for covert experimentation on an innocent unsuspecting public. Criminals, however, do want to rape you, steal your money, and torture you along the way to make themselves feel in control. Yes, I said the criminals can steal money using the satellite surveillance system! One of the earliest uses for satellite technology was electronic interfacing with computer systems. Wire and transfer fraud using satellite technology has been around a whole lot longer than most of the other things I've mentioned. If you've ever applied for or gotten a mortgage from any major banking institution, you're definitely going to need to keep reading...then change banks!

Weaponry is also a part of the satellite "surveillance" system being used by the CIA and NSA. I guess surveillance is kind of a misnomer since they can attack you with it as well as watch and control you. When my problems began occurring here in San Antonio, Texas, I spoke to an FBI agent that also happens to be a patient. As it happens, he has a friend in the CIA he was able to talk to, off the record of course, about what the system is capable of. Remember, the FBI is bound by constitutional limitations. They can track your vehicle with GPS, but they are not allowed to look into your bedroom or attack you with satellite weapons. As a matter of fact, the FBI agent I spoke with knew almost nothing about satellite surveillance and is recently trained. He received an education! In our initial conversation he said, "I'm with the FBI." If we had the technology to see inside your home, we'd be using it." In a later conversation and after speaking with a friend in the CIA, he verified that the system is capable of seeing you indoors using X-ray and has a variety of weapons on it. He went on to say, "It is a weapon of war for use abroad only and is on an intranet system supposedly inaccessible from outside the CIA or NSA." It is controlled using a government intranet system. However, it is obviously not inaccessible from those outside the system. The use of satellite surveillance abroad is strictly defined in "Executive Order 12333-United States Intelligence Activity" signed by Ronald Reagan, the President of the United States, on December 4, 1981. It also states that surveillance technology experimentation cannot be done without consent of the subjects being experimented on...for what it's worth.

Chapter 5

Non-Lethal Weaponry...Yeah, Right!

"A weapon of war for use abroad," my FBI patient stated. Then why was I being attacked in San Antonio, Texas? Maybe the CIA was using an old USA map from before the Battle of the Alamo! Texas was part of Mexico then, you know. Or maybe it was the criminals accessing their inaccessible system to destroy my life and the lives of people close to me. That must be it! I know that's it...and I know who's doing it too!

Remember, the imaging that allows you to be seen indoors is X-ray based. When we shoot X-rays of patients in surgery we wear lead shields for a reason. X-rays are harmful and a weapon by themselves. Long-term exposure to even low levels of radiation causes deleterious effects on the human body. These include premature aging, vision problems, organ damage, gastrointestinal damage, and cancer. The National Institute of Health (NIH) Website can direct you to some pretty good information on the long-term effects of chronic low-level radiation exposure. The criminals and non-criminals using the system would have you believe that the atmosphere absorbs all the radiation before a targeted individual is actually exposed to X-ray imaging. Not true! Firstly, the radiation associated with X-rays is ionizing radiation and not readily absorbed by anything. Hence, the lead shields we have to wear when shooting a patient's X-ray. Electromagnetic radiation, like solar radiation from the sun, gets partially absorbed by the atmosphere allowing you to sunburn and not ignite. Secondly, the mechanism of how the imagery and weapons alike reach the earth take atmospheric conditions into account. If you're thinking that rain and cloud cover can keep you safe from satellite surveillance, don't because it doesn't. Here's why: The satellite system creates a channel through the atmosphere through which its payload of goodies gets delivered to earth. Think of it like Santa coming unimpeded down a chimney bringing presents for all the good boys and girls. Only this Santa brings destruction, both physical and psychological. The channel is created by two parallel opposed lasers generated from the satellite itself that burn through the atmosphere leaving a clear channel between them. This is standard technology for all communication satellites except for satellite TV. That's why it will mess up during a thunderstorm. Nonetheless, I consider X-ray imaging a weapon, especially when those around you begin getting cancer from exposure to it.

The other weapons on the system are straightforward weaponry and not part of anything even remotely related to true "surveillance." They include electromagnetic radiation, microwave, laser, ultrasound, and particle beam. All are designed to cause bodily injury and incapacitate or destroy electronic systems. I'm going to be brief in explaining these weapons. You'll need a basic understanding of what they do to understand the rest of the book. For the technophiles out there, in depth descriptions of them can be found at http://www.globalsecurity.org, www. mindjustice.org and in a variety of declassified Department of Defense research articles on non-lethal weapons. One of those was mentioned earlier. Of note, in researching and developing these weapons, non-lethality was based on limited exposure of test subjects. The criminal element accessing these weapons will be using them 24/7, possibly for years, causing heart attacks, suicide and cancer. Hardly non-lethal in my book!

Electromagnetic radiation is predominately used to screw with electronics. It is also used to disrupt neural systems in the human body. For example, when exposed one might experience rhythmical twitching of various muscle groups, numbness or tingling, memory loss, fatigue, or loss of mental acuity. These are all meant to mimic possible physical disorders in the event you're not being verbally or auditory harassed at the same time. The effects on electrical and electronic systems are more pronounced and readily seen as abnormal. Many people think they're experiencing electrical problems with their household wiring or a haunting. Examples of these effects include lights turning off and on without touching the switch, cable boxes being fried repeatedly, your car computer shifting your transmission when it shouldn't be and slowing of your computer speed when you're researching the articles I've mentioned. The most pronounced evidence of electronic harassment is someone turning the power on and off to your entire home while you hear them tease you about doing it.

Microwave energy used as a weapon has actually been in existence for some time. Just as a microwave oven heats food up, the same is true for the human body when targeted by microwave weapons. The Army, CIA and NSA have all done exhaustive research on physical damage that can be produced with microwave heating up to and including death. The military's "active denial system" is composed primarily of supposed "non-lethal" microwave modalities. In the "Bio-effects of Selected Non-lethal Weapons" addendum some of the effects of microwave heating include disorientation, memory loss, delirium, convulsions and death. Of course, microwave weapons are used in a beam so the effects are dependent on the part of your body being targeted. A favorite criminal use of microwave weaponry is to cause acute, severe gastrointestinal symptoms like heartburn, vomiting of blood and blood in the stool. These are all caused by thermal changes to the cell lining of your stomach, esophagus, or intestines. For those being targeted by criminals using the system, the Army acknowledges the fact that metallic screen, several thicknesses on itself, will dissipate most microwave energy weapons. In studies researching the effects of microwave weapons, metallic insect screening worked pretty well as a conductive barrier to their efforts. This type of screening can be found at most home improvement stores.

Remember when you got your first laser pointer so you could look cool doing your presentation at the office or in class? The warning label on it said not to point at people's eyes, that it could cause damage. Lasers do cause all sorts of eye injuries and if you're being targeted by criminals using satellite based lasers you can bet they're aiming at your eyes. According to military research the effects on your eyes are threefold. They include dazzling or induced glare, loss of night adaptation and permanent or semi-permanent blinding. Targeted individuals may complain of eye burning, glare on windows they may be trying to look through, shadowing on window glass making it difficult to see out of, and an increasing time for their eyes to accommodate to darkness. Myself, and others being targeted, noticed early on our night vision steadily got worse as we were targeted. If you feel you're being targeted get an ophthalmologic exam. Laser injuries to the eye are often permanent and will show up on exam as burns to the cornea and retina. In addition to eye injuries, lasers also cause thermal damage to tissue in varying degrees depending on the type of laser and how it is pulsed at you. On the skin you may notice burns, hair loss, depigmentation and markings demonstrating the geometry of the beam. Long-term exposure to laser light, whether as a weapon or used as the guidance system for non-laser weapons can also cause skin cancer. It is a wavelength of light and can cause basal cell skin cancer in chronic exposure.

Ultrasonic weapons are another modality that has undergone extensive research for use as non-lethal weapons. Ultrasonic weapons and microwaves are similar in nature as are their effects. As ultrasonic beams approach the bandwidth of microwaves, they are capable of thermal injury. However, they are mostly used to exert physical pressure. For example, when used against the human heart muscle, asystole can be achieved by applying enough pressure in a pulse wave to stop the heart. This pressure wave can be effectively used on the entire human vascular system to retard or completely stop blood circulation. Arteries have muscular walls around them and are the body's high-pressure system. The pressure of the blood inside them and their design make them hard to collapse with extrinsic pressure. However, veins have lower pressure, no muscular walls and are very collapsible. Ultrasonic pressure applied to both the inferior vena cava and superior vena cava, the veins returning blood to your heart, can cause dizziness and unconsciousness in short order. The heart can only pump the blood it has coming in. When the supply coming in stops, the heart quickly reduces the amount of blood being pumped to the brain and you pass out. This is a favorite method of attack by criminals using satellite ultrasonic weapons. The symptoms begin with the sensation of an outside pressure against your chest or heart followed by lightheadedness and fainting. The criminals are hoping you'll mistake their attack as a heart attack; however, the pressure against your chest feels like it's coming from an external source. The same pressure phenomenon can be used to shut down your urethra and bowels making it difficult to urinate or have a bowel movement. Lastly, when used on the head, ultrasonic weapons may cause stupor, sedation, confusion and runny nose.

The worst weapon included in the satellite arsenal is called a particle beam. It consists of a beam of positrons or neutrinos directed in a line at a target. I'm no physicist, but declassified descriptions can be found on previously mentioned Websites that are scientifically complete. Particle beams were designed to destroy electronics but where soon found to have a great second use; they also destroy tissue! Upon impact particle beams also liberate X-rays exposing the targeted subject to radiation. In effect, being struck only once could possibly continue to cause you health problems years down the road. The take home message on particle beam is that it causes severe pain on impact and may keep hurting you after the physical pain subsides.

Some of this still, I know, seems hard to believe! If you choose to look further into it, the research and data is out there on these weapons. My descriptions are brief and in no way complete. However, I felt providing the reader with some basic knowledge of the technology is essential in understanding the rest of the book. Any internet or intranet system can be hacked into! The systems containing the nation's satellite surveillance and weaponry systems are no different. Non-government affiliated criminals are accessing one of our nation's most secret and terrifying weapons for their own agendas. All of these technologies I've mentioned have legitimate research with consenting subjects as guinea pigs. Targeted individuals who feel the FBI or CIA is experimenting on them are probably being attacked by criminals hacking into the system. Now, armed with the basics, you're ready for "the rest of the story," as Paul Harvey would say! This might read like a sci-fi movie script, but it is a true account.

Chapter 6

Back To San Antonio

I returned to San Antonio, Texas, in 1996 after completing four years of residency in Youngstown, Ohio. I was offered a couple of positions in Ohio and I had made some close friends that I really didn't want to leave, but San Antonio was home. My mother had gone into renal failure necessitating tri-weekly dialysis treatments and I wanted to be nearby. Mary and I packed up our meager belongings into a U-Haul truck along-side the Harley and left for San Antonio with my Isuzu Amigo in tow. I had gotten an apartment on the north side of the city a month earlier to move into upon arrival. After three days on the road we pulled into the Marquis at Deerfield Apartments at 3:00 in the morning. We slept in the U-Haul until 9:00a.m., when the office opened. At 9:05 we had the keys and the garage door opener as well as a grand tour of my one-bedroom efficiency. I later put Mary in a nearby apartment complex and began trying to start my medical practice. The job I had been promised several months earlier had fallen through so I was literally starting out with nothing.

The day we finished loading the U-Haul in Youngstown I had received a phone call from the physician in charge of the group I was supposedly joining. Bad news! Their group was merging with several other anesthesia groups to form one large super-group. He was no longer in a position to hire me. I would have to speak to another physician, the head of this new super-group, Rios Anesthesia. I phoned the Director of Rios Anesthesia to see about joining the group and was flatly rejected. They were looking for doctors with established practices not new doctors straight out of residency, he claimed. So here I was, back in San

Antonio with my degree, my training, no job and a lot of debt. Welcome home!

I started knocking on surgeons' doors and re-introducing myself to people who knew me as a technician. As work steadily grew into a pretty good practice, Mary and I grew steadily apart. She hated San Antonio, I knew that, but something else seemed to be going on. At first, I thought the move and being away from her family was bothering her. Her personality began to change, she became very temperamental and her anorexia began to resurface. In less than a year she wanted to go back to Ohio, with or without me. As I had mentioned earlier her apartment had been getting broken into, nothing stolen, just ransacked. On several visits I had found her either too emotional to be around or too somnambulant to keep awake. I wrote it off to the stress she was apparently undergoing and the poor diet she had fallen back into. Nonetheless, it wasn't long until she said, "I'm going back to Youngstown in thirty days, hopefully with you, but thirty days no matter what." On the thirty-first day her apartment was empty, her bags were packed and she was somewhere on the road back to Ohio. I didn't understand what her problem was at the time, but the future would enlighten me soon enough. One of the surgeons that started using me for anesthesia was my old friend, Harry Shelby. His wife, Cherlynn, was cracking the whip on him a lot more than she had been eight years ago. Apparently, during my time out of town attending school and residency, he had gotten caught attending to a young nurse's vagina behind his wife's back. He was still the heavy drinker and "good ole boy" I remembered, but his wife was usually included at happy hour now standing sentry at his fly. That was okay with me; Cherlynn is a decent woman trying to handle a bad situation as best she could I figured.

As our friendship rekindled, we began hunting and fishing together, as well as working together. During the first years of my practice I was damn-near living on his wife's friendship muffins. (No sexual pun intended!) She makes some damn good friendship muffins and I ate my weight in them every chance I got. Then I sometimes took some home for later! As time went on Harry and I became closer as colleagues and friends, or so I thought. His former mistress went on to marry an anesthesiologist, who suffered a similar fate to my own, amazingly enough, and was replaced by a new girl. At first he was a little more cautious about concealing his new girlfriend but over time became very flagrant about it. She did billing at the surgical center, where we did our cases, and did Harry on Tuesdays. You see on Tuesdays, Harry had no surgeries and no patients to be seen in the office. He would tell his wife that the day was spent doing paperwork. Actually her name is Jody, not paperwork, and most Tuesdays found them both at the Ramada Inn in North Central San Antonio. Coincidentally, in a city of over one million people they were using a hotel where the desk clerk knew who he was and they knew he was married. Oh well, as far as I know they're still seeing each other and his wife's none the wiser.

Even though Harry and I had some fun times together there was always something unsettling about him. He has a bad temper, but that's common among most alcoholics and never really troubled me. Everyone that has ever worked with him knows some days he loves you and other days he hates you for really no reason. I know his wife was trying to make him cut down on his drinking, so I figured the closer he got to delirium tremens the more hateful he probably was. For those of you unaware, delirium tremens, or the DT's, are a constellation of symptoms occurring with alcohol withdrawal. It starts with irritability and agitation and progresses to full- blown delusions and seizures if alcohol is withheld. But that still wasn't it. Something deeper in his psyche just didn't seem quite right. In my opinion, Harry's behavior as an alcoholic, an adulterer, a liar, and somewhat of a sociopath made me wary of him. As time continued, his evil nature would soon show itself.

Chapter 7

The Dirty Secret

In the State of Texas private investigators are licensed by the Department of Public Safety (DPS). This is the same department that issues your driver's license, concealed handgun carrying permits, security guard licenses and handles a physician's ability to prescribe narcotic medications. As a physician in the State of Texas, you need both a federal DEA number and a DPS number to prescribe certain medications. Nonetheless, to become a private investigator you have to submit to a background check, read a pamphlet, take a test and that's enough to get your license. Thus, if you weren't too much of a criminal before applying, you're eligible to be licensed to start your new criminal career as a private investigator. After speaking to several DPS officers, our state troopers in Texas, they really don't seem too happy about the Private Security Board being part of the DPS. Mostly, because of the aforementioned problem, private investigators usually amount to criminals with state licenses. Private investigators are supposed to conduct investigations under the same letter of the law as law enforcement, but rarely do. For those legitimate PI's out there, of course, I'm generalizing. I'm sure in most states private investigation is all on the up and up, but in Texas, we've got criminals with licenses! As a matter of fact, in San Antonio, a city well over one million strong, we have two state troopers assigned to overseeing the illegality of private investigation. That's two cats to watch three yellow pages full of mice advertising everything from background checks to following your spouse around to see who they're boning.

If you're interested, the Department of Public Safety in Texas has a great Website. Just click on "private security" and you can search by name, for whichever criminal, I mean investigator, who may be harassing you.

On Friday morning after putting a slew of ear tubes in little kids at the surgical center Harry Shelby laid a bomb on his surgical technician and me. Mando, his technician, and I had become pretty good friends and weren't sure what to make of the conversation we had with Harry that day. Pretty much out of the blue Harry confessed to being in tight with a private investigator named Frank Higgins. Actually, he is listed as Kenneth Franklin Higgins of KF Higgins and Associates according to his DPS bio. Harry beamed as he went on and on about the barely legal harassment type "investigation" he would do for him. He claimed he was former FBI and that they called him "the ghost." Harry Shelby's campfire account of this animal would make you wonder if he was going to materialize in your bedroom while you're reading this book. He went on to say, "I'm hiding Kenneth from my wife in case I ever want to use him against her in a divorce."

Mando had met "the ghost" on several occasions in the office. Not quite as enamored with him as Harry, Mando described him as a former FBI curmudgeon in his late sixties and somewhat of a jerk. Why Harry disclosed this to Mando and me was never clear in my head. Perhaps he was feeling guilty or maybe he was drunk. I'll never know. I do know that he turned him loose on me, my girlfriend, and our families with technology that he's not supposed to be accessing.

Every private investigative company licensed by the DPS has a data sheet listing their current and former employees. If you search his current list of employees it will read differently from the one I originally accessed. As they say, "the names have been changed to protect the guilty!" It's probably not uncommon for most businesses to have employees that are related. However, in KF Higgins's case, virtually all of his employees listed are relatives. Kenneth's wife, Katherine Byler Higgins, emphasis on the "Byler" has a brother, John "Chuck" Byler. He and his wife Susan, their three sons and their wives comprise the bulk of "the ghost's" investigative enterprise. Chuck Byler, in addition to working for "the ghost," also presents himself as a realtor for a realty company in Boerne, Texas, a suburb just north of San Antonio. As a matter of fact, the entire Byler family all live within blocks of each other in Boerne, Texas, probably at "the ghost's" request. They have endeared themselves to this small community, playing a very active role in the United Methodist Church of Boerne. Remember, the Bible plainly states "that the Devil can quote the scripture with the best of them"! The Bylers fulfill that prophecy to a tee.

They attend church on Sunday and praise God with smiles on their faces only to come home and sit in front of their monitors and invade people's privacy that afternoon. Truly, laughing with the sinners and crying with the Saints!

Another name worth mentioning off "the ghostly" DPS data sheet is Travis Howell. His significance will come later in the book. He works part-time doing surveillance for "the ghost" and full-time as a mortgage broker for Wachovia, formerly World Savings Bank. They do mortgage lending via a Telemarketing type of approach. One calls Wachovia, a broker is assigned, they take every scrap of your financial information over the phone including account numbers and balances, and you get a call back as to the status of your loan. The company looks like a military base nestled in the Hill Country of San Antonio comprised of thousands of six-foot by six-foot cubicles housing telemortgage brokers. I know this to be true; my ex-girlfriend, also a victim of KF Higgins, works for Wachovia as a mortgage broker. You'll see the relevance of this information later when we get around to the phrase "borrowing from the public."

I guess, like attorneys, private investigators fulfill a need in society. Most agencies probably operate within the confines of the law. However, the experience I've had is not of this type. Through illegal access to a satellite surveillance system, their actions can hardly be construed as investigative or surveillance. Our experiences have been attack, sexual assault, breaking and entering and harassment, all under the guise of an investigative agency. The main purpose of this book is to give you a peek at the tragedies that can occur when licensed criminals gain access to a government weapon. If you're not scared you should be! There's no escaping satellite surveillance and attack. Local law enforcement agencies won't believe you, the FBI doesn't know anything about advanced satellite surveillance and the agencies that do aren't going to publicize classified technology to help you. As Freedom From Covert Surveillance and Harassment quotes, "there's power in the knowledge that you're not alone."

Chapter 8

Priscilla's Nightmare

After practicing a year or so in a solo practice I helped form a conglomeration of anesthesia groups into a larger group called Meteor Anesthesia. As mentioned before, several groups had merged, forming Rios Anesthesia and now the remaining independent groups would merge to comprise Meteor. These became two rival and competing anesthesia groups, each consisting of about seventy physicians. I quickly became friends with Priscilla, a girl in her late twenties, who did billing and coding for Meteor. She had recently gone through a divorce and was living alone on the Northeast side of San Antonio. By this time I had built the house, intended for Mary and me, just north of San Antonio in the small community of Bulverde. Until recently my home was situated on four acres of wooded land with no neighbors to speak of; at least, none close enough to stop everything from being stolen as the house was built. My pet kinkajou and I moved into my 3800 square foot home in the country, enjoying dark starry skies and the popular nature wind we lovingly call a "hill-country breeze," lots of wildlife and little to no security whatsoever. San Antonio is in Bexar County and has a pretty good police department; however, Bulverde is in Comal County with only a Sheriff's department for our protection. They're great at writing traffic tickets, but anything else, and you're pretty much on your own. Priscilla began house-sitting for me and taking care of Zoe, my kinkajou, when I would travel back to Ohio. Living in the country, silence can make you hear all sorts of things. Surveillance equipment installed in your home while it's under construction can make you hear things too! At first Priscilla didn't have a problem staying nights in

Bulverde. She's fairly independent and doesn't scare easily. That would change almost overnight. At first she had claimed to sleep better at my house in the absence of sirens and dogs barking as in her neighborhood. Suddenly, she couldn't bear to be alone in my house, much less stay overnight. I thought the sound of white-tail deer hooves clip-clopping around the house or coyotes wailing may have had her spooked. It wasn't that at all. She had a hard time explaining exactly what had her scared of being alone in my house. On several occasions she had barely gotten Zoe fed before running out to her car, panic-stricken, burning rubber all the way back to San Antonio. Her best attempt at an explanation was that the house seemed open or was transmitting. I don't mean open like the doors were open, but open in a paranormal sense. She knew little about surveillance equipment at that time and even less about satellite surveillance and was describing what she felt as best she could. She was describing the low amplitude hum that both satellite surveillance and hidden microphones can emit, especially in a quiet country home. The sound is best described as a very faint buzzing similar to the sound of fluorescent lights, yet heard all around you.

But it wasn't just my house giving her the creeps! Priscilla was the first to notice the break-ins. Her house began getting broken into routinely with nothing ever stolen and a lot of damage being done. Her neighbors, once she met them, told her they had seen a white or silver compact car on several occasions parked in front of the house. A dark haired man in his thirties, they claim, was walking in the front door as if he had a key. They really didn't know Priscilla and weren't sure who was really supposed to be coming and going. Important message! If you don't know your neighbors...get to know them!

As it would turn out, the few neighbors I have in Bulverde had seen people breaking into my house as well. The damage being done at Priscilla's house was very peculiar. Doors and windows, as well as appliances were being taken apart and reassembled. Her microwave, refrigerator and oven had all been taken apart and re-assembled causing damage to all three. The appliances at my house were suffering a similar fate. Of note, the freezer and refrigerator doors had been taken off their hinges and holes drilled in their bases with a hole saw, allowing their contents to thaw and refreeze. During the course of a work day entire rooms had been repainted without her consent. Another important point: Don't leave sheetrock and matching paint around your house for criminals to use while installing surveillance equipment in your house! If they have to bring it with them it will increase their chances of getting caught. That is, unless your neighbors are part of it! Get to know your neighbors before they get to know you.

More troubling than the break-ins and damaged appliances were the people, like imbeciles, sitting in their cars on the curb right outside Priscilla's front door. On the occasions I would stay there, as we would get ready for bed, we both noticed a car pulling up and someone sitting in front of the house. She lives in a regular neighborhood and we disregarded it at first as visitors at one of the neighbors.' I began checking at 3:00 or 4:00 a.m. only to notice a person usually still sitting there. It sounds like radio frequency–based surveillance equipment if someone has to be right outside your home, right?

"I thought this book is about satellite surveillance," you're probably asking. It was, and it is. Remember, satellite imaging indoors is X-ray based, giving the viewer an X-ray image of you not the clear picture of a pinhole camera picked up by a receiver or routed onto the Internet. Criminals don't get aroused by X-ray images and until they master hearing your EEG processing they'll need microphones in your house to hear conversations. Once they're adept at using EEG processing to hear what you're hearing, the need for microphones will become obsolete. As for the person sitting in front of the house every night, staring out the window at him with a gun in my hand put a stop to that. Or at least, it made them hide a little better when they started using one neighbor's home.

Over time and seemingly unstoppable break-ins, Priscilla would notice something else in her house. The hollow interior doors were being taken off their hinges and ever so slightly shortened at the bottom, thus allowing one to look under the bedroom or bathroom doors with baseboard mounted pinhole cameras. Priscilla noticed something shaking or rattling in her bedroom closet door as well. We took it apart to find wiring, glue and a plastic mounting system housing a battery operated pinhole camera facing her bed from the always open closet door. This would be enough to start a sex crimes investigation by the San Antonio Police Department, but not until more people were involved and many more crimes were committed.

Chapter 9

Mallory

Mallory and I met around 1998 at a fashionable bar in the Lincoln Heights area of San Antonio called the Stone Werks, so named because of its past as a previously functioning cement quarry; It's smoke stacks are still in place hinting of its former industrial glory. Limestone quarries for cement making were a common industry for many years in the area. As neighborhoods grew around them the dynamiting of limestone had to stop and they were forced to move to a different area. In San Antonio we've mastered the art of turning limestone encrusted holes in the ground into bustling shopping complexes with upscale nightclubs. The Stone Werks was one of these. The upwardly mobile locals hung out there pretending to like Jaegermaister, partially smoking overpriced cigars and showing off their latest convertible BMWs. It's mostly an outdoor type of place and lies pretty dormant unless it's warm enough for a spaghetti string top.

Two weeks after meeting we began dating and remained inseparable through the next few years. At first things went great. Mallory was attractive, blonde, with a look akin to Nicole Kidman, as people would tell her. She had a pleasant personality and was finishing a BA in business psychology at Incarnate Word University. Her college graduation was one of our first dates and I knew then I was falling in love with her. She seemed to be doing the same. However, as with Mary, outside forces would intervene intending on destroying our lives.

One of our earliest dates was an outing to the rifle range to sight in my hunting rifles for the upcoming hunting season. Mallory is pro-wildlife and somewhat anti-hunting, so naturally anti-gun as well. After training her on the use of a Remington 700 Varminter

223, she began consistently hitting bulls-eyes at 100 yards. Her anti-gun sentiment began to subside with each successful bulls-eye and the day ended with her new experience leaving her feeling "empowered." "Empowering" and "proactive" were two of her favorite words she had gleaned from a quite extensive library of 1990's self-help books. Shooting wasn't her only first this day. This day would also be her first introduction to Harry Shelby, who was also at the range sighting in some rifles. An introduction we would both regret.

Several weeks later, by chance, we encountered Harry and his wife at an oyster bar in the Medical Center area. A popular place characterized by cold draft beer in schooners and crawfish by the pound. The Dry Dock Oyster Bar was a favorite lunch spot of both Harry and I. Or should I say, I would have lunch while Harry would stand outside the restaurant talking on the phone to his girlfriend. However, on this rare occasion Cherylynn was with him. I introduced Mallory to Cherylynn who in trying to introduce Harry was interrupted by Mallory, "Oh, I met Harry at the rifle range with John a couple of weeks ago." The silence was deafening and the look on Cherylynn's face was even more deafening. "Oh…is that right," she flatly replied. As a rule, I try to include the person I'm dating in my pastimes or interests. Harry, on the other hand, had long ago told Cherylynn that the rifle range was strictly for the guys. Of course, rifle range to Harry usually meant Ramada Inn with his girlfriend, thus explaining the no domestic uterus rule at the range. Cherylynn was not pleased that one of the guys had brought his girlfriend to the range and was quite vocal about that in the restaurant. I'm sure she was even more vocal on the ride home with Harry.

Harry became increasingly critical of Mallory and our relationship over the next several years. Most men, obviously including myself, found her quite attractive. However, Harry would repeatedly comment to me that he didn't think she was that pretty and stated "You could do better." I wrote this off to his repeated attraction to Hispanic women; Mallory, being blonde and blue eyed, wasn't the type of woman he usually pursued for a mistress. In retrospect, I think he was intentionally trying to steer me away from a relationship with her. In retrospect, I think he was trying to discourage me from a relationship with her as he was already planning his assault.

More so than previous girlfriends, I spent a lot of time with Mallory, frequenting her condo almost daily. She lives in a condo in Alamo Heights, near downtown San Antonio, so, to spare her the drive out to Bulverde, I usually went to her place. As with other women from my past, her place began getting broken into, appliances were disassembled and the doors and walls were cut into apparently for surveillance equipment. My being there posed a problem for the stalking that had also begun by this time. As Priscilla's ordeal unfolded and my house began to suffer multiple break-ins, I became more aware of my surroundings. The same vehicles seen in Priscilla's neighborhood were also being spotted driving around Mallory's condominium complex.

During our time together Mallory had been hired at World Savings Bank, now Wachovia, as a mortgage broker. Before her hiring, I had noticed people following me from her place as well as people following her home from mine. They were obvious but kept their distance. However, after her hiring their assault intensified on all fronts. The damage being done to her condo became extremely obvious. No longer carefully concealing their break-ins, mismatched paint mottled her bathroom walls, bathroom mirrors were removed and re-installed with cracks in them and furniture would be left out of place. These were minor in comparison to the changes occurring in her. The symptoms I overlooked as stress in Mary were happening again several fold in Mallory. Symptoms of control!

Harry and "the ghost" were destroying the woman I loved and would soon try to destroy my life for figuring it out. Attempts to talk to her about any of the problems proved futile. Her sudden heavy drinking and extreme emotional states she attributed to her job and the damage to her condo as normal wear and tear. It was easy at that point to assume she was part of whatever Harry's criminals were doing to me.

After discovering more about satellite based control I was able to see the true extent of her victimization. People being controlled don't realize they're being controlled and any attempt to enlighten them usually fails. The thoughts they have sound like their thoughts! Therefore, their actions help to victimize themselves and those around them unwittingly. Not everyone is controllable but Mallory is one of the unlucky subset of the population that is apparently totally controllable.

After the conversation I had with Harry Shelby in the OR about KF Higgins and Associates, I was fairly certain the harassment was coming from them. At that point I wasn't looking at it from a purely sexual assault point of view and thought there may be other reasons for our targeting. Any other reasons would be criminal as well, but I refused to believe that even Harry would go so far as to take part in sexual assault. I spoke to Mallory about Harry, the conversation, satellite surveillance and KF Higgins. It was like talking to a wall! She couldn't understand why Harry would want to target us and really didn't understand anything about satellite surveillance technology. I eventually got around to showing her KF Higgin's DPS data sheet and asked her if she recognized any of the names he had listed.

Despite her being controlled, the first piece of the puzzle went into place. "Yeah, Travis Howell works at World Savings. He does the same thing I do. He's a mortgage broker." Mortgage broker full-time, sex offender part-time, I wondered? She went on to describe him as a workaholic, married to Amy Howell with children and very successful at his trade. No kidding! Most of the brokers, Mallory included, averaged sixteen to twenty loans per month. Travis usually averaged forty to sixty loans per month. Her comment after that was even more interesting about Travis Howell. She was initially hired and placed on his team, as the boss wanted her to pick up his successful business tactics.

However, immediately after her hiring, he put in for a transfer to another building entirely to avoid contact with her. I repeatedly asked her if she had seen or gotten involved with any inappropriate banking business. She denied being part of anything illegal and wasn't on the same team with Travis long enough to know anything about his practices.

Chapter 10

Voices Of Terrorists

Convincing Mallory that we were under a criminal form of surveillance meant to destroy us proved difficult to say the least. I had pointed out damage to our homes caused by surveillance equipment installation and told her of people stalking us both. Hell, I had written down license plate numbers of people following me around her condominium complex, had them traced, and told her whom they were. She would always try to find a reasonable explanation to describe the stalking. None of them ever made any sense. Then, I tried explaining the voices! I had been hearing them harass me for quite some time, as had she, though she wouldn't or couldn't admit it. Now, when I say voices I don't mean God or angels talking to you in your head! These are broadcasts, via satellite by criminals, coming through anything that vibrates around you that will carry and slightly amplify sound. It is laser guided so your fan, aquarium, or running water can become the speaker through which your tormentors can psychologically and physically harass and terrorize you. In my case it is KF Higgins and Associates comprised mostly of his relatives, the Byler family. Long before ever talking to Mallory about this, I would lie awake in bed listening to them threaten to murder her or me. The harassment was mostly intended to deprive me of sleep, as I would drive to Mallory's at 3:00 a.m. to make sure she was safe. Harry and "the ghosts" were attempting to send me to work at 7:00 a.m. exhausted hoping I would kill a patient and lose my career. Harry's thinking was alcoholically simple; no career...no money...and no money—no way to do anything about his treasonous enterprise.

The broadcasts I first started hearing were conversations between the criminals, usually talking about Priscilla or Mallory, intended for me to hear. Comments like, "John's back home in Bulverde, go ahead and break into Mallory's condo," or "It's imperative that Dr. Hall think we're some kind of law enforcement if this is going to work" were made. The latter comment was made by Kenneth Higgins, "the ghost" himself. At that point I'm not so sure the criminals knew I was hearing them or at least knew how much I was hearing. For Christ's sake, they were using their real names in conversation with each other! The broadcasts quickly turned to a threatening and terroristic nature once they were certain I was hearing them. I began getting bombarded, 24/7, everywhere I went with threats. "We're going to murder you." "We're going to murder Mallory. "We're going to murder Priscilla or "We're going to kill your pets." I had on several occasions caught Mallory mumbling back to voices she was hearing in the running water as she would wash her face or brush her teeth. Several times I caught her talking to her bedroom wall or screaming at people in her condo that weren't physically in the room. I knew she was hearing the same criminal broadcasts. I had begun responding to them in the same way. They count on your vocal responses. It makes you look delusional which is their goal! Remember, you can respond by thinking back at your tormentors using a satellite system. They're actually hearing your thoughts before your vocal response anyway. Unless, as with us, you happen to live in the vicinity of your tormentors then they may be using microphones to listen to your conversations, as well as the thoughts that immediately precede them. Mallory, not believing anything I told her about satellite surveillance, was responding out loud at her house and mine. Others were hearing them too. Priscilla began hearing their voices transmitted through her computer speakers at Meteor Anesthesia. She knew a little about satellite capability and knew the situation with Mallory so "the ghost" was trying to make her appear delusional enough to be fired. Delusional people aren't credible witnesses! One of her co-workers began hearing her "spirit guide" talk to her through her computer as did her babysitter and several other friends. Mindy, Priscilla's co-worker would come to work telling her of the "spirit guides" talking to her and her friends over her home computer. Priscilla kept silent, knowing it was KF Higgins and Associates. Mindy's babysitter, Amy, would later lose her father to a massive heart attack in McQueeny, Texas. In itself, that wouldn't be all too strange of an occurrence. However, for several hours before his heart attack he stood in the living room conversing with the Devil. He even called his wife into the room in an attempt to get her to hear the unseen Devil, telling him it was his last night on earth. She never heard the voices he swore were in the room with them. His body was carried away by law enforcement the next morning. The "ghost" made good on his promise with an ultrasonic induced heart attack via satellite. I would hear the criminals later claim this was an accident; however, you don't accidentally get targeted by satellite and accidentally tormented and murdered by its weapons.

Another person in my circle who was hearing the criminals was Jason McGiver. He is the former owner of the gym where I currently work out and is actively pursuing an acting career. The reason for his targeting was several-fold. I spend a lot of time at the gym and after being targeted, the criminals found a victim rich environment among the young women also working out there. Secondly, I had confided in Jason what was going on and was using the gym computer for research. Lastly, Jason has an attractive wife with a great rack which would get him targeted at home as well as the gym. Under Jason's watch the gym would have several break-ins; as with other locations, things were tampered with but nothing stolen. Since I was using his computer, I would assume one of the reasons for breaking in was to install a key-logger on the computer. The one found on my home computer was from a software company called DoMex. He had also heard the criminals conversing about me as their broadcasts came clearly through the vibrations of a cooler cabinet used to refrigerate sports drinks. Jason would soon start hearing his name being called from an air conditioning vent in the hallway outside his bedroom. Of course, this necessitated that he pull the covers off himself and his wife while he looked for someone inside their home. Pulling the covers gave the stalker the chance to view his wife in the nude. Jason was also being attacked with satellite weapons causing muscle twitching, parasthesias, and gastro-intestinal bleeding. The modus operandi of these criminals is to make the male in a relationship seem delusional, hoping to tear apart the relationship, isolating the woman for easier sexual assault. Luckily, Jason's marriage survived his torment, I'm sure, allowing his wife a safer existence than if divorce had left her home alone. The divide and conquer practices of the criminals tormenting us stems from good military training. Isolation usually begets easy victory, or in this case, easy victimization. Amazingly, one of KF Higgins's employees, "the ghost's" brother, Robert Higgins, was a Lieutenant Colonel in the Air Force. This is not coincidence!

Ultimately the isolate-and-victimize strategy would unfortunately destroy the relationship between Mallory and me, leaving her in the vulnerable position they desired. Attempts to explain our situation to her were useless. The criminals had found an attractive girl, totally controllable, to victimize psychologically and physically. As I said before, the controlled do not realize they're being controlled. I presented her with digital recordings of her ranting, as well as, recordings of her condo being broken into while she was home. She would be controlled into ignoring them or dismissing them. The conversations were usually forgotten by the next day. I juggled the positions of both boyfriend and security guard for Mallory for several years. Keeping watch on her condo when she appeared controlled or drugged, to prevent the criminals from breaking in while she was home. The battle was made more difficult by some condo's being made available to the criminals and neighbors willingly assisting them in their assault. The demise of our relationship would leave them unrestricted access to repeated rape, with Mallory having little to no recall and no recourse due to drugging and satellite control.

Chapter 11

Neighbors From Hell

As I said before, get to know your neighbors before they get to know you. It was our experience that our neighbors were helping "the ghost" in victimizing us both knowingly and through deception. Private investigators will tell people just about anything to gain their confidence and assistance, including producing false ID's as one type of law enforcement agency or another. They may be willingly helping criminals invade your privacy or be fooled into allowing receivers or cameras to be mounted on their homes around yours, thinking they're helping a legitimate agency. Trust me, the FBI is not going to ask your neighbors for permission to mount pan-tilt-zoom cameras on their house to watch you. However, criminals posing as FBI or police will! Never underestimate the stupidity of the public; many people will believe whatever story the criminals present, especially if there's a financial incentive. Mallory was followed from my home in Bulverde almost every visit by people parking up a side road by my house. They sat patiently in direct view of one of my neighbors, following her the second her car would exit my driveway. After a police investigation began and I noticed his involvement, the house went up for sale and he abruptly moved out. If you live in a newly developed neighborhood as I do, vacant homes and homes under construction may be used to observe you. It's easy for the criminals to hide from police there as long as they're gone before the construction crews arrive at first light.

After confiding in Mallory about hearing the audio harassment of satellite surveillance, another piece of the puzzle presented itself as to the definite identity of our tormentors. I stepped out onto the patio of her condo at about midnight to get some fresh air and enjoy a cold beer. As I stood hidden from the condominium next to hers by her over and under washer/dryer unit, I overheard a conversation. Not a broadcast, but two people talking next door. Rene Calhoun, a dental assistant, was renting the condo near hers from William and Jane Bryant, a couple from Ariton, Alabama. She had caught a small-statured Hispanic male creeping behind the privacy fence of her patio towards Mallory's bedroom window. Upon questioning him, he told her he was an FBI agent watching Mallory and me. A request for ID prompted him to change his story. "I'm with KF Higgins Investigations; we're watching that blonde girl and her boyfriend," he said. As I bolted from around the washer, Rene backed away from the stranger onto her patio and the man scrambled backwards away from me into the darkness. Not long after that encounter Ms. Calhoun moved to Austin, Texas and the condo was sold. Property appraisal records would later show that William and Jane Bryant owned condos on either side of Mallory. Both were sold after that occurrence and two more were purchased, this time on the second story overlooking both the front of Mallory's condo and the rear entrance to the parking area. As of this writing, they still hold ownership of the latter two condominiums.

Two of her other neighbors would later prove to be suspect in assisting "the ghost" in his stalking of Mallory. Directly across from her living room, about twenty feet across a small courtyard, lived John Rankin. Long before ever hearing their harassment or noticing the stalking, I had noticed something peculiar about the back of his condo facing Mallory's. The mini blinds in his window had been cut at the sides in several places for camera placement facing her living room bay windows. The aging aluminum bay windows in her condo were non-curtained with older mini blinds in place.

At night, with interior lights on, her living room could easily be seen through the closed mini blinds. A camera twenty feet away would be great for a peeping tom, which I suspected him to be. He would turn out to be much more! As we watched television in her living room one night I heard a rustling in the shrubs below her bay window and a faint tap on the glass. I bolted through the front door only to be staring face to face with a thin, dark-haired woman. She let out a scream and ran across the courtyard, clutching the device she intended to mount outside the window, only to hide behind the patio of John Rankin. I would later identify this woman as Leslie Byler, a Boerne school teacher and wife of Jeffery Byler, a relative and employee of KF Higgins.

Another incident occurring with Mallory's neighbors involved Juan and Sarah Bocanegra. Juan, a former Ranger American employee and his unemployed wife, both in their late twenties, live in the building adjacent to Mallory's condo. I always found it odd that they would walk their dogs in the courtyard and intentionally stand directly in front of Mallory's living room windows. On several occasions, after hearing a noise in the shrubs, I would look out of Mallory's blinds to find Juan staring back at me. His face practically pressed against the glass. Juan and Sarah knew I was dating Mallory. Hell, I couldn't help but say hello to them as they were standing in front of Mallory's windows practically daily. There is grass in front of their condo as well, but they always stood by Mallory's. Other than a quick "hello," Mallory really didn't speak to this couple much either. Her parents, however...that was apparently a different story! Her parents had started coming over during the work day doing minor repair work and painting her aging condominium. The family dynamics between Mallory and her mother and step-father can be described as strange at best. Her family is definitely not anywhere close to the Ozzie and Harriet ideal of the all-American family. When they came over to work on Mallory's condo, she wanted them gone before she returned home from work.

Unknown to us, Sarah Bocanegra had been coming over to her condo to visit with her parents as they painted. Pretending to know Mallory better than she really does, her parents trusted her and thought she was looking out for their daughter. She was looking all right but not in Mallory's best interest. Controlling a victim's parent goes back to the isolate and victimize doctrine that these criminals ascribe to. Mislead and control a person's loved ones so they have no one to turn to when they finally do realize they're being victimized.

As I mentioned before, I had already begun sitting in my vehicle around Mallory's condo when she would appear drugged or exhibit odd behavior. The Bocanegra's knew me and my vehicle, would wave when they drove by. By this time they had lived next door to Mallory for several years, no longer new to the complex. On one particular occasion Sarah would find Mallory's parents painting and repairing some shutters. Striking up a conversation, pretending to be a close friend of Mallory, she expressed her fears about someone stalking their daughter. Without giving the name of the supposed stalker, she described the vehicle and handed them a piece of paper with a license plate number. The information was immediately relayed to Mallory and following down the chain of command, I guess one would say, to me. Sarah Bocanegra had described my truck and given my plate number to them as the alleged stalker. The same Sarah Bocanegra I would say "hello" to almost daily at Mallory's living room window and wave as they passed my vehicle on the street. Juan and Sarah were working with "the ghost" to victimize Mallory as I thought all along. Her voice would come up again on a recording of Mallory's condo being broken into. In an attempt to collect evidence against the criminals I began placing voice activated digital recorders hidden around Mallory's condo. These would eventually lend evidence to the sexual assault that was happening with assistance from her neighbors.

The tactic employed by Harry and "the ghost" did succeed in alienating me from Mallory's parents. After speaking to them, it was easily seen that they were not only misled but controlled. They were more alarmed about me invading the privacy of a girl I had now dated for eight years then her possibly being raped. I showed her step-father signs where her condo had been broken into, where her microwave oven had been disassembled, and told him of finding her apparently drugged with Rohypnol and amnestic of me being there. On several occasions she had blackouts and thought I was there in bed with her where I had not been. Remember, I'm a physician and am well aware of the effects of Rohypnol and GHB, drugs currently used by rapists to block the memory of their victims. Her step-father's reply was brief and controlled. "Sarah Bocanegra watches her place too close for anything like that to be happening." I was shocked. Non-controlled parents would have wanted police involvement at the mere suspicion of their daughter being raped. Her parents disregarded it completely.

Chapter12

Rohypnol And Satellite

As a physician, I've seen the devastating effects of Rohypnol, the "date rape drug" when used by rapists to block the memories of their victims. Although a woman may realize she's been raped, the drug, usually surreptitiously spiked in a drink, denies the ability to identify her attackers. In states that border Mexico it's been a huge problem due to its easy availability. Rohypnol and its equally sinister cousin GHB have both been banned from use in the US due to their use in drug assisted rape. However, they're both available without prescription across the border in Mexico and through illicit foreign pharmaceutical Websites. For years they were undetectable in the urine of rape victims; however, of recent, tests have been made available that will detect them for up to 36 hours post-ingestion. The FBI and local law enforcement agencies have stiffened the penalties for drug assisted rape, re-classifying them as aggravated sexual assault, a felony.

Rohypnol combined with satellite control is an even more menacing problem. In most cases, the drug is placed in the drink of the victim in a bar room setting. Odorless and tasteless, it goes un-noticed until the victim awakens to find signs of assault, with little or no recall to initiate a legal investigation. If that's not horrible enough, compound the problem with someone already the victim of satellite mind control. No longer would the victim have to be abducted or raped in a parking lot; they're drugged and raped at home. The police are of little help in this scenario even if the victim suspects rape. Since you haven't left the house and have no recall of the attackers, they pretty much disregard it. That is, if the victim is brave enough to call the police in the first place, knowing their recall is limited or often attributing it to a nightmare. Such was the case with Mallory. After much deliberation about why we were being targeted, it finally came clear to us that the sexual assault was their main motive. As I mentioned before, the stalking and attacks escalated after Mallory's hiring at World Savings Bank as a mortgage broker; especially after identifying Travis Howell as both an employee of KF Higgins and one of Mallory's co-workers. After finding her in an apparent drugged state on several occasions, I began checking her bottled water, drinks, food and whatever else I felt could be tampered with. As far as I'm concerned, rape would be the only reason to drug a woman with Rohypnol. Indeed, I found bottled water with needle punctures in them, tea bags with a corner snipped off and glued back together, and frozen dinners that had been opened and re-sealed. I personally witnessed her drink several bottles of water out of her refrigerator then begin to get drowsy, making odd sounds and displaying bizarre behavior before falling asleep. Her odd behavior and suspected drugging is what prompted me to start placing digital recorders around her condo and sticking around after leaving her to catch the intruders. On several occasions I received phone calls from her, apparently after being drugged, unable to hold a conversation making odd noises and repeatedly accidentally hanging up on me. After two of these calls I immediately drove to her condo to find her in a drugged state and totally unaware of my presence for several hours. The next day she would ask me, "What was I doing when you arrived?" I had banged repeatedly on her bedroom window to wake her at 8:00 pm on a Sunday evening to get her to open the front door. She had no recollection of me arriving or the next three to four hours of my being there. I made several attempts to convince her to let me take her to the emergency room which she refused. On one of these visits not only was she found obtunded and amnestic, but her kitchen shutters were found wide open and music was blaring loudly from a kitchen radio. Her back door and kitchen window open to a secluded patio area that was not part of her alarm system. It seemed to me the area was set up to be broken into after the drugs would take their effect. I stayed with her that night, I'm sure angering whoever had worked so hard to get her drugged and prepare her place for an easy break-in.

My attempts at keeping her rapist at bay by watching her condo on the nights she seemed drugged did seem to be working. Obviously pissed off, employees, or should I say rapists, working for "the ghost" began harassing me as I sat in her parking area. Vehicles would either follow me around the complex or make repeated passes by my truck staring at me and at times shooting the finger at me. I knew they were trying to scare me off so they could break into Mallory's condo. What they didn't realize is that I was writing their license plate numbers down. There's no perfect crime. Satellite comes close, but not when you combine it with in-person harassment using your own vehicles. Unbelievable! These idiots were actually using their own vehicles to stalk Mallory and Priscilla as well as in following me. One night I scared a man in his thirties away from her living room windows at 3:00 am. I saw him again at a similar hour, creeping around behind her condo and followed him to his gold Ford Expedition, parked along the dark rear entrance to her parking area. The entrance was overlooked by condos owned by William and Jane Bryant. His plate number would return ownership to Lt. Col. Robert Higgins, his son Eric Higgins was the driver and person I had seen. Robert Higgins, listed as an employee of KF Higgins and Associates, gave me irrefutable proof that "the ghost" was indeed behind the torture we were experiencing.

Trying to convince Mallory that she was being raped and drugged was pointless. Between the satellite mind control and minimal recall she had as a result of the Rohypnol, it was like talking to a wall. However, she did notice several odd things that she readily admitted to me. She had noticed a sudden increase in bacterial vaginal infections and yeast infections that had never occurred before. Certain medical conditions can pre-dispose women to frequent yeast infections, but this wasn't the case. She has none of these risks factors. However, frequent or rough sex, especially with multiple partners, is also a risk factor for recurring vaginal infections. At this point in our relationship our sex life was non-existent due to the stress placed on us by KF

Higgins and Associates and as far as I knew she was seeing no one else. At last, I convinced her to at least see her gynecologist rather than calling in to have medicine prescribed over the phone for the infections. Her doctor had been calling in Diflucan tablets and Flagyl for her infections without actually examining her. With the infections recurring with growing frequency, I gave her no choice but to make an appointment and have an examination. Once the appointment was scheduled, I was sure to speak to her gynecologist before her visit to express my concerns about the infections and the possibility of drug-assisted rape. Before her appointment I would once again find her in a drugged and amnesic state, this time with hand shaped bruises across each buttock and marks on her breasts and legs. She thought she had bumped into the corner of her dresser...I thought she had been raped. "The ghost" would do everything in his power to keep her from getting a vaginal exam, making clear the reason for their assault.

Chapter 13

Murder, Attempted Murder

Before I admitted to Mallory I was hearing harassing broadcasts by our criminal tormentors, she had asked me about having children. During a conversation I vividly remember in her kitchen, she expressed the desire to start a family. "My mother's wondering when we're going to give her some grandchildren." I was flabbergasted! I had been waiting for her to ask me that for years! "Of course I want to have children with you; I wanted that years ago," I replied. She went to her bathroom and brought her birth control pills to me which I promptly threw in the trash can. "It's going to be a big responsibility" she said. "I know, I'm ready," I replied. My first wife had two boys from her first husband. I loved being a father, and now the thought of having my own children with a woman I loved more than life didn't sound like extra responsibility. It sounded great! We made love in every room of the condo that day, my mouth and hands caressing every inch of her body in unrestricted desire. I knew the effects of her birth control pills hadn't worn off yet, but what the hell, a little practice couldn't hurt! After the pill had worn off we made sure to have sex daily. She conceived in several months. I was ecstatic, but not for long.

Assuming I was doing the right thing, especially with a baby on the way, we had the conversation about the true extent of the satellite harassment I was hearing. I told her it was Harry Shelby and KF Higgins harassing us, the same Dr. Shelby that had supposedly been my friend and her surgeon. At one point, over the years, he had performed a tympanoplasty on her left ear to repair a hole in her eardrum that had impaired her hearing. Obviously, this was before I knew he was invading our privacy and taking part in sexually assaulting Mallory. It makes me sick every time I think about the fact that I trusted him to perform surgery on her! The comments I received back from her during our conversation were not what I wanted to hear, but not surprising either knowing the extent of her mind control. I knew she was hearing them harass her as well but couldn't admit it. Having caught her on many occasions having a conversation with her bedroom wall was a dead give-away. Nonetheless, she attributed every thing to schizophrenia on my part. Notwithstanding the employees of "the ghost" I had caught in her complex, their plate numbers verifying their identities and one of her co-workers working for them. I was schizophrenic! I thought, being pregnant, I would be able to overwhelm their control over her with facts and reason, if not love. I was wrong. She decided to have a medical abortion, killing the twin fetuses inside her, believing I had gone crazy. It would be the first of two abortions over a six month period. Besides God, the State of Texas and I consider this murder because she was tricked and threatened into these abortions.

Around the time of the first abortion one of the digital recorders I had hidden in her condo recorded the criminals breaking in while she was home. On a Saturday afternoon she began acting bizarre and drowsy after drinking bottled water that had been in her refrigerator for several days. She asked me to leave at 3:00 pm as she wanted to lie down and take a nap. I obliged and turned on the recorder hidden under her stove in the kitchen before I left. Apparently one hour later the recorder began recording. Mallory's bizarre behavior while drugged is clearly audible. Usually calm and collected, the woman you hear is screaming, banging pots and pans around and making animal noises. Her screen door opens from the patio multiple times as male voices are recorded behind her ranting: "Frank's a freak! Get out of my life! Get out of my house! You're not supposed to be here!" A male voice responds, "Frank's not the freak, you're the freak, Mallory." Another male voice tells her, "Go fuck yourself!" As the screen door opens again amid the pandemonium, Harry Shelby's voice clearly asking, "What's going on?" It sounds as if Mallory escapes to the patio only to be carried back in screaming, "Go away! Go away! Leave me alone! Leave me alone!" almost in a chant. As the intruders are dealing with Mallory, in a scared and drugged state, the doorbell rings. The voice of Sarah Bocanegra can be heard. "Can't you do something about her?" She asks as she goes through the kitchen cabinets looking for the recorder. Mallory's screams fade off into the living room and bedroom muffled by Sarah and male accomplices still looking for my recorder. "I found it! How do I turn it off?" she asks. A male voice responds, "Just start pushing buttons until it goes off." To this day Mallory thought she was taking a nap and having a nightmare. Finally armed with the identities of the stalkers and some evidence of their breaking in, I began to make plans for law enforcement involvement.

While once again Mallory had no recall, at least we had her screaming "the ghost's" name as he and his criminals broke in to assault her. Transmitted broadcasts could also be heard as a female voice told her, "Frank wants you to drink more of the juice in your refrigerator." She was obviously still too lucid and hard to handle from the dose they had gotten into from her water.

As I prepared to go to the police, we would both have attempts made on our lives. I took the digital recorder to a sound studio to have the background noises taken out of the recording and the voices brought forward making them clearly audible. After picking up the disc they prepared for me I noticed the hood of my truck shaking violently as I drove down the highway. The bolts to the hood latch had been partially removed causing my hood to fly up into my windshield on the highway. Luckily, I wasn't injured nor was anyone else and a police report was filed. They messed up and they knew it!

After the abortions and after the recording was made, Mallory began complaining of more infections. A medical abortion consists of a shot to kill the fetus, not a dilatation and curettage, so that wasn't the culprit. What I heard on the recording was! Amazingly, the wives of the criminals know their husbands are committing rape and help them commit it. I knew the Byler wives were assisting in the surveillance, but was surprised to hear Sarah Bocanegras's voice in Mallory's condo helping commit the sexual assault.

Having cancelled a prior gynecologist appointment, this time I threatened Mallory that I would drive her there myself. She scheduled another appointment! She left work at noon the day of her appointment to meet her parents for lunch before her 3:00 exam. During lunch she had left a Diet Coke in the console of her Volvo sedan to sip on her way to the doctor's office. In route she was overcome with a "shaky" feeling, nervous and trembling as a man in a truck tailgated her honking his horn. Upon arrival she had a blood pressure of 190/145 and was tachycardic with a heart rate in the 200s. Her gynecologist asked her is she had been having "rough sex" noting the tears in her vaginal walls. She refused hospital admission for the hypertension and came home, relating the whole story to me. Having had an attempt on my life, I assumed the same was done to her. I was right! Harry Shelby, being a physician like myself, knows the effects of the drug Epinephrine. The same drug that can save you during a heart attack can also give you one when you're not. Medical personnel have been murdering each other for years with Epinephrine. The most notable was a Dr. Swango that managed to kill several of his patients with Epinephrine before finally being caught. I immediately got a urine sample from Mallory for testing and collected the remainder of her Diet Coke from the car. Harry and "the ghost" intended for her to have a heart attack and a resulting car accident while driving to the gynecologist. One of the two would have certainly killed her and a routine autopsy does not include testing for metabolites of Epinephrine. Had she been successfully murdered, the autopsy would've simply shown myocardial infarction or motor vehicle accident as the cause. After explaining to Mallory the effects of Epinephrine, she consented to a urinalysis by Quest Laboratories which indeed came back positive for normetanephrine, the metabolite of Epinephrine. It was 140 points over the normal range. Harry and his criminal cohorts had raped my girlfriend, killed our kids and tried to kill us. As I set out to get law enforcement to help us, they set out to discredit me!

Chapter 14

San Antonio Police Department

Priscilla, now all too aware of and what was happening to Mallory and me, noted yet another break-in. This time an antique chest was destroyed. Holes were drilled into her refrigerator and something was rattling in her bedroom door. We took apart her bedroom door to find a pinhole camera mounted in plastic, the veneer carefully glued back over to appear like a knot in the wood grain with the small lens in the center. The wires dangling from the camera could be heard rattling as we moved the door back and forth. Her entrance door appeared to have been removed at the hinges damaging the frame and replaced with mix-matching screws. The police were called and yet another generic report was generated with no action taken. After playing Priscilla the recording of Mallory's assault, we decided to go a step further than calling another useless beat cop to the scene. After all, her last report didn't even mention the finding a camera in her bedroom. She was determined to help me save mine and Mallory's life. While most women would feel some compassion for another women being brutally raped, I guess it doesn't exist among the women in the Byler family, happily assisting in their husband's sex crimes. We decided to call on a patient and old friend, Tom Fulgate, the head at the Sex Crime Unit, in the San Antonio Police Department.

Seven years earlier I had mentioned to Tom that Mallory was acting strange and that we both seemed to be getting stalked. No official report was taken at that time as I wasn't sure of the identities of the criminals. This time I went to the police with a recording of Mallory screaming Frank's name, two attempts on our lives, a camera out of Priscilla's bedroom, and a fist full of police reports for breaking and entering. Before consulting Tom I decided to make an attempt to talk to Harry and "the ghost" in person. Call me crazy! I thought I would appeal to whatever goodness might be left in their evil souls to stop their assault on us. I wanted to be a father and a husband not a martyr to the cause of satellite surveillance and the government's failure to protect us from their own weapons. I met with Harry at a Bar and Grille called Texas 46. In front of Gord Smith, a Canadian citizen, and friend to us both, I told him of the abortions and asked him to call off the assault he had perpetrated on us through KF Higgins and Associates. Clutching a pistol hidden in his pocket, he denied any involvement or even knowing "the ghost." He went on to say, "I'm sorry about the abortions and I know you want children with Mallory and Mallory alone." By this time he hadn't seen or spoken to either one of us for several years. Except for having watched us, he wouldn't have even known we were still together. Several days later I went to KF Higgins' home at Fair Oaks Ranch, Texas. Upon arrival I was greeted by a man in a sedan claiming to be Kenneth Higgins. I guess the senile "ghost" forgot that I know what he looks like. The idiot that took this assignment, a much younger man, told me I wasn't welcome in Fair Oaks and threatened to shoot me if I didn't leave. "We're not doing anything," he replied when I told him to stop sexually assaulting Mallory and Priscilla. "The ghost," not the same poltergeist in person as he is via satellite, had apparently sent John Byler, Jr. out to scare me away in the same vehicle I had seen his son Brennen Byler stalking Mallory's condo. He followed me out of Fair Oaks and on my way back to Priscilla's house and attempted to call me on my cell phone, a number he shouldn't have known. I returned to Priscilla's to find a message on her home phone: "This is Kenneth Higgins...I understand John is trying to get a hold of me...have him call me back at this number." I couldn't believe these imbeciles had gotten away with disrupting our lives for this long.

I drove to the downtown substation of the SAPD to talk to Tom absolutely sure as to the identities of the criminals. Minimizing the satellite surveillance part of the story, I presented the evidence I did have of the break-ins, the assault, the hidden camera, and the threats. I didn't want to jeopardize getting an investigation under way by confusing poorly informed local law enforcement officials about the satellite part of their assaults. Hard evidence speaks for itself and I knew any crazy talk of satellite involvement would get me disregarded as a lunatic. Tom remembered me talking to him about the stalking several years earlier and listened patiently as the rest of the story unfolded. After hearing what had been happening since our last conversation, Tom summed it up pretty well.

"This is so out there, it's got to be true." Assuming the video equipment was being installed to record the rapes for online Web sites, he put me in touch with Immigration and Customs Enforcement (ICE) a part of the Department of Homeland Security. The rest of the investigation he placed in the hands of the SAPD Vice Squad. Some Vice Squad detectives went to Priscilla's home and took statements as well as the camera into their possession as evidence. The recordings, pictures of Priscilla and Mallory, and the names and addresses of KF Higgins and Associates were given to ICE. After interviewing Mallory, the Vice Squad handed the investigation back to the Sex Crimes Unit to be handled by them and the ICE Agents.

This investigation is currently on-going and the wheels of justice aren't spinning fast enough for my liking. However, at least the local law enforcement knows what's happening to Mallory, and who's doing it, which is protection in itself. If "the ghost" and his employees hold true to form they'll screw up again and get caught in the act. It's easy to remain anonymous harassing people with satellite, but when you start breaking in and assaulting them in person you're eventually going to be caught.

Chapter 15

The Set Up

After getting SAPD involved in our own plight, the frequency of the break-ins and sexual assaults began to wane. This was too little and too late for Mallory after having suffered multiple rapes and two abortions that will haunt her forever. "The ghost" now turned his attention to discrediting the only person who truly knew the facts about their crimes...me!

Harry Shelby, an alcoholic, adulterer, and now rapist and attempted murderer, maintains a self-illusion of being a pillar of the community. Credibility, being a valuable weapon in combating this type of crime is very important and he realizes that. In his delusional world that he himself and "the ghost" called "The Shelby CIA," he is unquestionable. The only reality in his world that scares him exists in his wife Cherylynn. She knows absolutely nothing about his other world, and he would risk prison before admitting any of it to her. Greed is mostly to blame. Harry's money is his personality and he would rather risk losing everything than watch her walk away with half of it in a divorce. She had almost divorced him for cheating; she most certainly would divorce him for rape! That being said, he instructed KF Higgins to begin a campaign at discrediting me with hopes of the investigation being dissolved. When not being controlled, Mallory does have recall and "the ghost" was hoping to kill her rather than watch and control her for the rest of her life. Discrediting me would be their attempt at saving themselves. Again, Harry's plan would be alcoholically simple; ruin my career and my finances and prevent me from helping Mallory. If the police dropped the investigation they would continue with their sexual assaults and possibly murder.

"The ghost" thought he had figured out a way to accomplish both her murder and discredit me in one fell swoop. Being an anesthesiologist, I'm an easy target. Addiction rates are high among anesthesiologists due to the easy access to drugs we use in the workplace to anesthetize patients. One in particular is Fentanyl. An analogue of Demerol, Fentanyl is one hundred times the potency of morphine and used extensively in anesthesia to render a patient pain-free during surgery. It also happens to be a favorite of drug addicted anesthesiologists! The chemical properties of Fentanyl make it bio-available through just about any route. It can be injected, swallowed, snorted and even absorbed through the skin due to its high lipid solubility. Fentanyl, like other narcotics, has side effects specific to the class of drug that are indicative of its use. Most noticeable are constricted pupils. Many anesthesiologists gauge whether a patient is still narcotized with Fentanyl by examining the pupils. If the patient is slow to come out of an anesthetic, reversal agents can be given to reverse the Fentanyl and thus the pupilary constriction. Other significant side effects include chest wall rigidity making ventilation difficult and nausea. There is a reason for the quick pharmacology lesson. On her way to work Mallory noted a feeling of pressure constricting her chest and throat while driving. The pressure would eventually make her pass out at the wheel in her car, luckily after she pulled over onto the shoulder of the highway. After returning to consciousness she returned home and called in sick; unfortunately, she was a victim of satellite based ultrasound. She described her symptoms to me as a feeling of pressure against her chest that felt "external" or as if it were "coming from the outside." She had also noted her pupils looked abnormally small after using a particular lotion she placed around her eyes when applying her cosmetics. The fainting episode precipitated her telling me about the lotion which apparently she had noticed for several days with each use. It's apparent they were trying to murder her with an MVA and make sure she would test positive for Fentanyl on autopsy. If their plan had worked, she would have been murdered and I would have been suspect in providing her the drug. I think they were hoping to murder her and get me charged with manslaughter. Two birds...one stone. It didn't work! I took the lotion from her for testing and we replaced the toothpaste, cosmetics, and anything else that could have been tampered with. Their plan would be verified several days later when I too was drugged.

At the time of the second attempt on her life she was still recovering from the second abortion. She was still bleeding abnormally heavy several weeks after the abortion shot. Almost passing out at work, she left early arriving at my house pale and tachycardic, indicative of acute anemia from the weeks of bleeding. While she filled my toilet with blood clots I could hear the criminal's broadcasting their laughter through the vibrations of the bathroom ventilation fan. Obviously, they were hoping she would bleed to death. I suspected that she had retained fetal products in her uterus, often a cause of prolonged bleeding after an abortion. Afraid of undergoing a D & C to remove the products, she refused to contact the doctor that had administered her shot at the Women's Choice Clinic. In fear for her life, I decided to speak to the doctor myself hoping he would convince her to be seen. She eventually was diagnosed with retained fetal products and given a second abortion shot causing her to expel the remnants and halt the bleeding. However, the conversation I had with her doctor would begin my financial hemorrhaging as well.

I had known the doctor since before I became a physician. Well respected and a good surgeon, he's one of the few gynecologists in San Antonio still performing elective abortions. This was when the procedure started requiring practitioners to wear Kevlar vests (bullet-proof vests). Most doctors stopped performing them. During our conversation about Mallory's bleeding I decided to confide in him the reasons for the abortions to begin with. I thought I could trust him and told him our story in confidence. I guess being a moron isn't reserved only for "the ghost." I had forgotten that this doctor is also very good friends with Harry Shelby. The two of them were partners in the ambulatory center where I had worked as a technician. He would report the conversation to Harry, who would arrange to have me accused of delusional behavior by the Methodist Hospital in San Antonio. As it turned out, one of my partners in Meteor Anesthesia Group, Dr. Solomon Cohen, also a long time friend of Harry's would assist in the accusation. I had long respected Dr. Cohen for his contributions in Vietnam as a medivac chopper pilot; his heroic deeds are mentioned in the book *Ripcord*, a story about an overrun firebase in the AShau Valley written by Keith Nolan. He was the last person I would suspect to help ruin my life up and I was learning a valuable lesson I had forgotten. Trust no one on the battlefield of satellite surveillance, especially other physicians.

I arrived at Methodist Hospital at 7:00 a.m. prepared to do anesthesia for a 7:30 a.m. case expecting a typical day. Upon arriving to the holding room for a pre-operative visit to a patient I was approached by Dr. Cohen asking to speak with me in private. This in itself wasn't too unusual as we were partners in Meteor Anesthesia and often talked privately about political problems within the group. We both essentially disliked the CEO running Meteor and would talk about his shortcomings in running the group. This was different! Acting nervously and with tears in his eyes, Dr. Cohen asked me to accompany him to a private room to meet with two other physicians. One of them was a retired anesthesiologist and former addict now heading up the impaired physician's group. I guess after you find God, they don't mind you preaching to the choir! Dr. Cohen possibly knew he was helping set me up as they questioned; "Is it true that you think you're under satellite surveillance or something?" I was speechless! They informed me that an appointment had already been made for me with a psychiatrist for an evaluation that day as Dr. Cohen asked me for a urine sample to test for drugs. He said that my urine sample would be taken to "his lab where he is the director, so nothing could go wrong." Suspecting that I was being set up by three of Harry's friends, I refused the appointment and the urine test with my privileges suspended that minute as a consequence. Literally, within the hour, Dr. Cohen would call my secretary graciously, volunteering to take over my "more lucrative spinal cases" in my absence. That comment is in the official record from Methodist Hospital, and in itself, suggests a set up. Mallory had just been drugged with Fentanyl several days prior to my inquisition so I knew what they were going to find in my urine. I drove straight to Walgreen's after leaving the hospital to get a urine test kit to test myself. Like Mallory, I had been drugged with a lethal combination of drugs probably meant to kill me, and when they didn't, ruining my career seemed like the next best option. Moreover, had Mallory died in their attempt to murder her, they would have needed me to test positive to help bring a manslaughter case against me. They missed again! I had long since stopped drinking or eating anything that had spent anytime in my refrigerator without my being there. Later that week, according to a friend working as a surgical technician at the Baptist Hospital, he claimed to have been asked by Dr. Cohen to Google John Fleming's article, "The Stalking Menace of Satellite Surveillance." Interesting!

Chapter 16

Delusional Or Not

The Methodist Hospital System, fulfilling their duty in cases like this, temporarily suspended my privileges pending drug testing and a psychiatric evaluation. Gordon Jackson, the non-physician CEO at Meteor Anesthesiology Group, would within the hour send letters to every other hospital system in the City of San Antonio suspending my privileges at these institutions as well. I sat at home that day greeting DHL Truck after DHL Truck bringing me certified letters notifying me of my suspended privileges. The letter from my own group, Meteor Anesthesia Group, seemed to be pre-written in expectation of my refusal to comply with the testing and evaluation already set up for me. Amazingly, Dr. Cohen was listed in a certified letter from Meteor as my peer advocate in the matter to whom all of my correspondence would go. I would ignore several calls from him that day on my cell phone, a number I had never given him in the first place. I retained a lawyer and began to comply with the demands from Methodist Hospital to be reinstated. My attorney would inform the attorney representing Methodist Hospital that my case was one of illegal surveillance and a set up over the crimes perpetrated against Mallory. Arrangements were made for my drug testing, psychiatric evaluation, and peer review meeting to regain my privileges.

The psychiatrist, Dr. Christopher Tilken, is apparently the "go to" guy for medical practitioners in San Antonio accused of impairment. The appointment my initial inquisitor had made on my behalf was at his office. So, naturally, knowing I had been set up, I tried to find a different "shrink" in an attempt to get a fair shake. Everyone I called referred me right back to

Dr. Tilken saying, "He's the doctor that usually handles you medical guys." Great! Begrudgingly, and with little choice, I made my appointment with Dr. Tilken, and the psychologist he referred me to for psychological testing. I would have to complete a day of psychological testing before approaching Dr. Tilken for the verdict on my sanity. The psychologist I had to see fits the expectation of what you imagine when you picture a psychologist. A sixties throw-back, with torn-up jeans and sandals, this man knew Mallory and me from the "Stone Werks," a restaurant and bar where he drank every Thursday night. At one point he had even asked Mallory out. I hadn't even actually seen the psychiatrist yet and I was already dreading the outcome. Nonetheless, I let him administer the MMPI (Minnesota Multi-Personality Inventory) test to me and looked over the Rorschach blots so he could tell me how much I hate my mother and how my father spanked me when I was little. My psychological testing was read as stone cold normal and I got to move up the ladder to the psychiatric evaluation. The physicians that had set me up initially had made an appointment with Dr. Tilken for me as you recall. Obviously I was apprehensive about seeing the person that, in my mind, could be part of the whole plan that "the ghost" had laid out for me. As I found out later, other physicians before me had been set up as well and a psychiatric evaluation was always instrumental in their downfall. Tilken, being the doctor that "always" handled medical professionals made me especially nervous. I entered his office for my appointment with one of my handy digital voice activate recorders in my pocket, figuring the conversation between us would eventually be heard by the FBI or some type of law involvement. The meeting initially consisted of the usual "how do you feel about your mother" psychiatric jargon and progressed to the story about Mallory. He was hoping to assert that my delusions of surveillance were the result of a deep depression over Mallory's abortions. One problem...I had already reported the surveillance happening before either abortion had occurred! Strike one! The questioning then turned to my knowledge of surveillance tactics. After all, what should an anesthesiologist know about surveillance? In my case, quite a bit. I had dealt with some FBI and organized crime issues when I lived In Youngstown, Ohio. I never said I'm perfect. Strike two! Then the incriminating question came up: "Have you ever or are you currently using anabolic steroids?" Earlier, Dr. Cohen, my peer advocate, (yeah, right!) had called my attorney accusing me of being on anabolic steroids. Grasping at straws, with a negative drug abuse panel and normal psychological testing, he claimed, "I must be in an anabolic steroid delusional state." Why would they ask about steroids, you're probably wondering? "The ghost" and his employees had gone through my house with a fine tooth comb on many occasions. During one of their break-ins they came across a shoe box in my attic with relics from my body-building days in my 20's which included dried up vials of steroids. They should have looked at the dates on the labels; it would have saved them the embarrassment of that accusation. I replied honestly to Dr. Tilken's questioning about steroid use and submitted to a negative urine screen for steroids to the tune of $600.00 out of my pocket. He then went on to ask pinpoint accurate questions about the symptoms that occur with satellite weapons attacks. "Do you hear voices around you, harassing you? Do you ever have numbness or tingling in your feet or hands? Do you ever feel pressure against your chest? Do you ever feel burning like your being attacked by unseen weapons?" Hmmm! I felt like asking, "Do you ever wonder how the anal sex in prison is going to feel like for helping people rape my girlfriend and kill our kids?" But I didn't. Instead, I just said Hell no!" "Do people really think they feel that stuff?" "That's crazy!" Dr. Tilken gave me a nice middle of the road open-ended evaluation. He agreed I wasn't delusional, citing my normal psychological testing, only to summarize in his last paragraph that everything could still be the result of an unknown or not as of yet identified drug toxicity. The door was being left partially open for "the ghost" to somehow get something in me that they could screw me with.

Fresh from psychiatric evaluation, I appeared before the peer review board of Methodist Hospital for my confidential hearing. Upon my arrival, none other than Dr. Harry Shelby was in the parking lot with his Hispanic girlfriend having a meeting of his own during her lunch break. Of course, he was getting a different screening than I was about to get! He never saw me get out of my truck and walk in the building as he exited his girlfriend's mini-van and sped off in his truck. My attorney attended the meeting with me but wasn't allowed in the proceedings. Any consultation with him would require me to step outside the meeting room then rejoin my inquisitors with his advice. This line of questioning was aimed at minimizing the fact that another physician was responsible for my predicament. On face value, I agreed with my wise peers that an ex-boyfriend of Mallory's certainly must be the culprit of our harassment. One older physician on the panel, however, was certainly in on what was really going on and decided to let me know that. Out of left field, he asked, "Dr. Hall, what is Echelon?" Luckily, my mind kept my mouth form saying "Go to hell!" My response instead was, "I think it's an information gathering system." But in my mind I said to myself, *make sure this moron's name is in the minutes, because that question didn't just come out of nowhere.* My privileges were reinstated and I began practicing again as well as continuing in preventing Mallory from being murdered. I practiced medicine for over a year before my next hurdle surfaced. Unbeknownst to me, the Methodist Hospital had notified the Texas Medical Board of my suspension. Over one year later the Board would exercise their right to investigate me and incidents surrounding my loss of privileges at Methodist Hospital. Naive of the way the Texas Medical Board operates, I assumed I would be treated fairly by a board of my peers possibly even helping me with my criminal tormentors. Wrong again! The Board would serve mainly to open the door even wider for "the ghost" to attempt a crowning blow to my career and keep himself out of prison for the crimes committed against Mallory.

Chapter 17

Bleach And The Texas Medical Board

What do bleach and the Texas Medical Board have in common? They've both been used by "the ghost" to ruin me over the last couple of years. A year after hurdling the Methodist debacle I received a package in the mail from the Texas Medical Board announcing their investigation into my loss of privileges. I spoke to their attorney informing him that I had successfully jumped through all of the hoops that Methodist presented and with all of their concerns met, had been practicing for well over a year. He informed me that despite a good outcome at the local level the Board still retained the right to investigate a physician to determine if they're in violation of the Texas Medical Act; a lengthy legal document poorly understood by most lawyers and apparently specifically written to confuse all physicians. The Board asked me for a written narrative of why I had lost my privileges and retained all of the records from Methodist Hospital pertaining to my case. I retained yet another attorney, this time a young women who apparently specializes in Medical Board litigation. As it would turn out an attorney is almost useless in dealing with the Board. They answer to no other authority and their decisions are apparently pretty well made before they ever meet with the accused and hear their side of the story. Nonetheless, I spent some more money on an attorney and was scheduled for what the Board calls an ISC (Informal Show of Compliance) or mini-inquisition composed of a three person panel selected from the full Board. The ISC panel hears the case and recommends an action to the full Board that accepts or rejects their recommendation. Notice that I said the ISC panel hears the case; they absolutely do not listen, they hear!

The Texas Medical Board consists of physicians, clergy, and non-medical individuals meant to represent a cross section of the normal population. Physicians are appointed to the Board by the Governor of the State of Texas. Doctors that are good at what they do practice medicine. Those not skilled at practicing medicine teach and those unskilled at both apparently make great candidates for appointment to the Board. Over the years, the madness that goes on within the Texas Medical Board has been the subject of much controversy. Touted as the most corrupt and inept Medical Board in the United States, they're currently being sued in a class action lawsuit by AAPS (American Association of Physicians and Surgeons). They're alleged to under react to verifiable serous issues and overreact to anonymous complaints filed against physicians, usually by other physicians, with something to gain by screwing up someone else's career. According to them, their sole purpose is to ensure the safety of the public by policing bad physicians. This seems to be best accomplished by not subjecting the public to those physicians appointed to the Board itself! Being that there is no recourse beyond the Board for a physician within their grasp, horror stories abound in Texas about doctors losing their careers based on petty, if not falsified, facts.

Not having had issues with the Board before, I awaited my first ISC believing a panel of educated peers would be hearing my issue. Believe it or not, I thought the Board might actually provide some insight into solving my problem with an investigative company sexually assaulting my girlfriend and jeopardizing my career to cover their crimes. After all, the Board also uses investigators when compiling all of their data for hearings against physicians. I was educated as to the callousness and lack of caring of the Board in short order. Their goal of protecting the public certainly didn't apply to protecting Mallory or me. As one of my future attorneys summarized it, "The Board feels there are too many doctors in Texas. It's easier to incriminate the physician and take your license than investigate and rectify the real problem." This is a statement coming from an attorney who has both worked for the Board and against the Board.

As I awaited my ISC, the attacks on Mallory and I escalated with my home being broken into almost daily and employees of "the ghost" following us everywhere we went. I noticed my pets and I were feeling ill practically every day and my socks and shoes had a sudden strange odor. After coming home late from work one night, I discovered why! That morning I left for work feeling ill, breathing with difficulty and vomiting small amounts of blood. Upon arriving at home I began drinking water out of my tap, only to notice the green washcloth I had wiped my mouth with was turning white. Drops of water spilled on my shirt were leaving white spots as well. I had noticed earlier that my hair was turning white with each shower I took at the speed of light. I now know why. I was being bleached! My water softener company, Ecowater, came out the next day to check my softener and test my water. The garage, housing the softening unit, had to be ventilated as the serviceman replaced the resin that had been contaminated with approximately five gallons of household bleach. Their report details the overpowering smell of chlorine and the burning and stinging of his hands as he changed out the resin. We both agreed that I had, yet another, attempt on my life. Or could it be something else?

Household bleach, sodium hypochlorite is an alkaline solution having a pH of 10.5 – 11.0. The lower the pH of a substance the more acidic it is, while the higher the more alkaline. When bleach is mixed with an acid it liberates chlorine gas or chloramine gas which acts as a lung irritant causing pulmonary edema and chemical pneumonia. When bleach is exposed to moisture it decomposes to hypochoric acid, an irritant. Wait a minute! Our stomach has both acid and moisture in it. So what happens when another physician and his criminal investigators make you drink it? Any physician can open up a toxicology textbook and figure this out! I figured it out with absolutely no help from the Texas Medical Board, who was informed that I was being poisoned with bleach from the beginning. While I was being poisoned, they would sit around scratching their heads pretending to not know what bleach does once ingested into the human body. Small amounts of bleach will slowly raise the pH of your body to an alkaline state while eating away at the lining of your stomach and esophagus. Hence, the reason I wound up having an endoscopy when I woke up one morning in a bed full of bloody vomit. I was diagnosed with erosive gastritis and esophagitis. In large amounts, you became acidotic from the decomposition of the bleach into acid. Either way, when ingested, bleach makes you sick and it seriously screws up your gastrointestinal system. Poisoning someone with bleach is attempted murder in itself but "the ghost" and Harry Shelby had another reason for it as well.

Part of their attempted murder of Mallory and their discrediting of me involved surreptitious drugging. Mallory had been drugged to facilitate rape as well as drugged to hasten her death. For their set up to work in discrediting me, they would have to rely on a third party to find me positive for something illegal after a credible accusation. The accusation had already been made. The people I had caught and recorded victimizing us wanted it to appear as if it were all in my head. This would also put into question the capabilities of the satellite surveillance system they were using. They were hoping that all of it would appear to be the result of severe delusions from my alleged use of anabolic steroids. Only one problem with that scenario! I didn't test positive for anabolic steroids and my psychological testing was normal. What's a "ghost" to do? Again, that's where the bleach comes into play. The body excretes many drugs by acidifying them in the urine. If you're trying to set someone up by drugging them, you would need them to be positive whenever they may be asked to test. Getting a third party to accuse someone of being on drugs and test them isn't as easy as breaking into their home and putting drugs in their food or water. You would need your victim to stay drugged as long as you can to ensure a positive urine test when it finally gets asked for. Bleach solves that problem! As the body is chronically alkanalized by daily bleach ingestion the speed at which drug metabolite excretion occurs is severely lowered. Thus allowing someone to drug you periodically and have you retain enough of the metabolites to test positive on a screen, for double or triple the time that your body would ordinarily excrete it.

With an upcoming board hearing, "the ghost" needed me to be positive for something in order to ruin my career. In their minds, that would be their only way of getting away with being terrorists and rapists. The Board could have and should have figured all this out just as I did! Their failure to do so, in my mind, imparts some culpability on them for our attempted murders and Mallory's sexual assaults. They would find if easier to call me drugged or delusional than call the FBI for a legitimate investigation of the facts.

Chapter 18

ISC # 1

(Informal Show of Compliance)

As my attorney and I prepared my defense for my upcoming inquisition by the Board, the attacks, harassment, stalking, and break-ins escalated to an alarming level. Harry and "the ghost" knew I was going into this meeting with a clean drug screen, a normal psychiatric evaluation, and over a year of medical practice without a bad occurrence or lawsuit. They were trying desperately to drug, assault, or incriminate me in any way they could before the meeting. "You've got to get him to do something stupid and get arrested" I would hear Harry broadcast almost daily. The Bylers doing the majority of the harassment and break-ins were getting irritated over the fact that I couldn't be controlled as easily as Mallory. Obviously, if I could have been controlled like her, you probably wouldn't be reading this for I would have been put in jail long ago! The stalking had evolved to a direct physical harassment by employees of "the ghost" driving circles around me in their own vehicles, flippant of police involvement. Several nights at Priscilla's, we could hear people walking around on the rooftop in an attempt to terrorize us. On one occasion we saw a Hispanic male jump off her roof into the backyard, running to the safety of one of her neighbor's yard who also happens to be a private investigator. Remember what I mentioned about getting to know neighbors? Two young men in their early twenties had been following me around Mallory's condo and Priscilla's neighborhood, obviously too young to be private investigators, but they made themselves painfully obvious. One evening they made the mistake of allowing me to see them pulling into the driveway of one of Priscilla's neighbor's, adjusting a camera mounted to their carport facing Priscilla's house. Their black Oldsmobile Bravada was parked three houses down at a home owned by Ross Byler, a local Methodist minister who actually lives in Mallory's neighborhood. That evening, as I left Priscilla's to go to Mallory's, the two men slowly drove past me making intentional eye contact with me. They waited for me up the street as I left Priscilla's. I purposefully led them around the neighborhood to be sure I wasn't imagining their intent. As they followed me around the neighborhood, I quickly notified the detective who was helping me with the problem and told him of my two young ignorant stalkers. "Let them follow you to Mallory's and then call me." He said he could have them pulled over for stalking." By this time I had allowed them to follow me right back to their house where I very obviously got out my vehicle and wrote down their license plate number and their home address. Obviously, told of my call to the police, the two would-be "James Bonds" pulled back into their driveway and went inside their house.

An anonymous letter to the owner of the house would rekindle the spiritual relationship between the Minister and God. Within one week of its receipt, the stalkers were sent packing and the house sits vacant to this day.

The satellite weapons attacks became more and more severe as police involvement precluded them from drugging us as easily. I had begun to routinely check food and drinks left at all of our residences for evidence of tampering. Murder from the sky would seem like a better alternative to "the ghost" after seeing I was no longer afraid of appearing delusional to the police. As a matter of fact, it was at this time I spoke with an FBI agent about the surveillance and the attacks. He revealed the capabilities of the satellite system through a friend of his currently with the CIA. Now knowledgeable of the X-ray and weapons capability of the system, he was sure that it is controlled by an inaccessible, government only intranet system. However, he did agree to be of assistance.

As for Priscilla and me, a gastrointestinal doctor would first be of more assistance! Microwave attacks had left us both vomiting blood and passing blood in our stool. On Mallory's front, both sexual assault and satellite attacks were occurring with growing frequency. An oval red mark had begun to appear on her forehead, the result of twenty-four hours per day laser guided mind control and microwave hearing technology. A basal cell cancer was excised from the area. This cancer is unusual for a woman in her early thirties, who rarely, if ever, spent time in the sun. After its excision the same oval shape marks began to appear elsewhere on her face as "the ghost" would try other areas of the skull to infiltrate her thoughts. No longer anonymous, with police and FBI at last notified, "the ghost" couldn't risk Mallory having any recall of her horrific events.

My inquisition fast approaching, the attacks on me became almost unbearable. Audio harassment and directed energy attack were being doled out around the clock simultaneously. "He's got to look like he's on drugs," I heard Harry telling his criminals. "Attack him when he tries to shower and don't let him sleep, he continued." Actually, worse than being totally sleep deprived, they would stop their attacks at 4:00 or 5:00 a.m. hoping I would sleep through my alarm once I fell asleep. "He's not impaired or anything" I heard "the ghost" tell Harry one night. His reply was "then you need to impair that mother fucker!"

Being a little older than me and having seen "Midnight Express" a few too many times, Harry and "the ghost" have a pre-conceived notion of what a drug addict is supposed to look like. They wanted me reporting to work sleep deprived, dark circles around my eyes, smelling of body order with greasy hair. I guess they didn't realize most drug addicts these days are clean cut and professional looking, especially among physicians. One exception is alcoholism. Years of heavy drinking does change a person physically with tale-tell signs. Chronic drinkers often display reddened faces, telangectasia, or spider looking veins on their face, a bumpy looking nose called rhinophyma and skinny arms and legs with an out of proportion potbelly. Harry should know this; he sees it in the mirror everyday! I knew they were planning on drugging me again however, the satellite attacks had become so constant and severe I wondered if they would get their chance. I sat in the OR one afternoon, a patient asleep on the operating table, as Harry attacked my midsection with a particle beam while audibly threatening me through the vibrations of our monitoring equipment. "I'm going to put you in renal failure like your fucking mother," I heard, as my kidneys were relentlessly attacked. Harry and I had still been working together when my mother received a kidney transplant several years before after years on dialysis. I found out later that one of our tormentors, Chuck Byler, claims to be a lung transplant recipient. If true, it certainly did not bestow any compassion on his part toward my Mother, both my parents were being controlled and attacked as well.

Watching everything I ate or drank and carrying all my personal hygiene products with me, I awaited my ISC. I had now replaced my shoes and sandals several times over due to bleach being poured into my shoe plants. A combination of bleach-soaked skin and satellite microwave had given me severe burns on my heels and toes making it difficult to walk on many days. Fine pieces of metal had also been embedded in my shoes to augment the burning effect of microwave in my feet. If you've ever put anything metallic in a microwave oven, you know the effect! When I would notice my shoes had been tampered with I would replace them. It's difficult to watch all of your belongings all of the time, they get to everything eventually when you're being watched twenty-four hours a day.

My attorney and I reported to Austin, Texas to answer whatever questions arose from the panel assigned to my case. Customarily, the panel was comprised of two physicians, one non-physician member, a stenographer and the Board attorney.

One of the physicians on my panel happened to be a psychiatrist. Supposedly a well respected forensic psychiatrist from San Antonio, this man is widely published and held in very high esteem, especially by the AAPS, who specified him by name in their lawsuit against The Texas Medical Board. By several accounts, he has never failed to provide a psychiatric diagnosis befitting of whatever punishment the Board is looking to dole out to someone. He fits my previously mentioned Board member criteria perfectly! There is only one other psychiatrist in the State of Texas whose nose is imbedded deeper into the circle of the Texas Medical Board than this guy, and he gets mentioned later. I had to condense several years of tragedy into ten minutes for the bemusement of my inquisitors. As I explained the rapes, surveillance, break-ins, and the set-up I would see the dumbfounded looks on their faces. Remember these doctors didn't get appointed to the Board by being geniuses in their field. They knew, or at least pretended to know, very little about even the most basic of surveillance tactics, and any knowledge of satellite was non-existent. The shrink on the panel, we'll call him Sigmund, wiped his balding head and said I have one question: "Do you really believe that a private investigator can break into your house, hide a camera in the wall, and repair the damage all in an eight hour work day before you return home?" The belittling tone in his voice infuriated me! My fist clinched tight, I held back the answer that I really wanted to give. This man held in such high regard had obviously never read a newspaper much less perused the assortment of pinhole cameras that can be purchased online or in electronic shops. Hell, even Home Depot was selling "nanny cams" for a while! Nonetheless, I held back my anger and played the role of the uneducated slave that the Board has come to expect. Kneeling at the steps of the ivory tower, I replied; "I don't know what I believe." I figured there was no sense arguing with them. The meeting adjourned with the panel unsure of what to do with me. Several days later my attorney notified me that their decision was to do nothing and that would be the recommendation to the full board who would ultimately decide my fate. My attorney seemingly enamored with the Board attorney, told me that he was a really nice guy and looking out for my best interest. "Everything's going to be okay" she said. I immediately went back to San Antonio, stock-piling on KY jelly for what was surely on the way! The Board attorney was looking out for my best interest...I doubt it!

Chapter 19

Penetration All Around

By this time Mallory was still being raped, Priscilla's house was still being broken into and vandalized, my office was broken into and patient files tampered with, and I was awaiting a good screwing from the Board. They wouldn't disappoint me! Two months after my ISC, where no action was recommended to the Board, my attorney called me on my cell phone. While two months prior she was sure everything would be okay, her voice on this occasion was somber and worrisome. "We've got a problem," she said. According to her, for the first time in Board history, they didn't follow the recommendation of the panel or their own attorney. Before making any decision on my case they wanted yet another psychiatric evaluation by a Board-appointed psychiatrist. Actually, I had seen a Board-appointed psychiatrist, before my first ISC, named Dr. Silberley, a South African gentleman who apparently travels around the United States performing forensic evaluations for numerous State medical boards. A sort of forensic psychiatric "hired gun" I guess you could say. He had given me a clean bill of health, stating that I had a legal problem going on, not a psychiatric one. I guess that wasn't the answer the Texas Medical Board was looking for, so I was asked to see yet another shrink at the Board's request and at my expense. The doctor they appointed was Dr. Randall Myer, a psychiatrist at the teaching facility of Scott and White Hospital in Temple, Texas.

I made an appointment with Dr. Myer at his earliest convenience, sending him all the information he requested to supplement that previously sent to him directly from the Board. A late afternoon time was scheduled as Temple is a two-hour drive North of San Antonio and I had morning cases already scheduled.

Priscilla accompanied me on the trip for moral support, both of us expecting the worst. Our expectations were met! I arrived to be greeted by an irritable little psychiatrist, angry that he was busy that day and had no resident to do his work for him. In a medical teaching institution it's easy for physicians to become complacent and lazy since interns and residents do most of the work. On this day he was actually having to see some patients and was obviously disturbed about it. His first words to me were "I've got to tell you...I'm not your treating doctor and I am not looking out for your best interest...I'm here to write a report for the Board." If I could have walked out of his office I would have! That comment alone told me everything I needed to know about the evaluation I was going to receive.

He began with the usual baseline questioning about family relationships and history of family mental illness. We then progressed to the standard memory task of counting backwards, remembering three words and interpreting common phrases like, "What do people mean when they say; 'Don't cry over spilled milk'?"

If you've never gone through a psychiatric evaluation you might be interested in getting one, if for no other reason, than to see what a useless specialty it really is. Most people with severe mental disturbances go without treatment due to lack of insurance. Depression rates are still high in spite of new medications, and their techniques of evaluation haven't changed since I was in medical school in the 1980's. Unless you are seriously mentally ill the diagnosis is purely a judgment call on the part of the psychiatrist with no true empiric tests or symptoms to rely on or prove the diagnosis.

After the basic late 1800's psychiatric exam, we delved into my real problem of stalking, surveillance, and sexual assault. I put more evidence in front of this psychiatrist than I had from the two previous doctors. We went over ADT alarm records of the alarm break-ins at my house, police reports, photos of appliances taken apart and statements from other victims experiencing the same problems. Our meeting ended with him asking for permission to speak to my father about the issues. I agreed to allow him to speak to my father which he did several days later. I forewarned my father of the call. My father was surprised to see a supposed excerpt from that conversation in the report that followed.

He didn't merely misrepresent my father's words in his reports...he blatantly falsified them! If the board was trying to create a diagnosis for me to avoid investigating the real problem, they definitely found their man in Dr. Myer. His report was a frantic attempt to find a diagnosis where none existed. He was truthful in one regard; "he wasn't looking out for my best interest."

In reading his evaluation, I felt it didn't look too condemning through most of it. He mentioned, item by item, the evidence of vandalism, the numerous police reports, and the reason for suspecting Harry Shelby and KF Higgin's investigators. He quarreled about the ability of PI's to break-in and install surveillance equipment without the home owner's knowledge of it and totally dismissed satellite surveillance capability altogether. I guess he never watched the news highlighting Anthony Pellicano's 110 counts of breaking and entering and improper video charges. Pellicano was one of the most successful private investigators, harassing the rich and famous for other equally rich and famous clients. He then went on to dismiss the computer generated ADT reports documenting many of the intrusions into my home, citing his inability to interpret their data. For those of you with alarms systems, you can request written copies and occurrences of when your monitored alarm system has gone off. It documents time of entry, location of the breach, the phone number of the police department called, and often the badge number of the officer responding. I could read these reports as could most people, but they were beyond the scope of this highly educated psychiatrist. He claimed I was defensive on my psychological testing having been previously read as "normal" by a psychologist and two prior psychiatrists. Lastly, he completely lied about the conversation he had with my father claiming that my father, "thought Priscilla had some secondary gain by maintaining my belief that I was under surveillance." A comment my father absolutely denied, which I have no trouble believing, since the conversation was recorded in its entirety. Dr. Myer summarized his report stating that I had somehow slipped my delusional disorder past two previous psychiatrists and lucky for the Board, he was here to bring it to light. On another note, Dr. Myer charged me $2,000 which was to be paid in full, before seeing me or writing my report.

I entered my second ISC with negative drug testing, a negative metabolic steroid screen, normal psychological testing, two normal psychiatric evaluations, and one damaging psychiatric evaluation. In addition, there were more police reports of the break-ins and the positive identities of KF Higgins employees and their traces of their license plates while stalking us. The panel, this time, completely disregarded the sexual assaults on Mallory and focused on how I obtained the identities of the stalkers. Any comments I made about attacks on Mallory were met with harsh rebuttals.

They seemed to have forgotten that the sexual assaults and the abortions were the reasons I had lost my privileges at the Methodist Hospital in the first place. The meeting went on for fifteen minutes, with their questions de-emphasizing Mallory's peril and focusing of my supposed delusional disorder. This scholarly group, despite my tutorial in toxicology, couldn't understand my having been poisoned repeatedly with bleach either. With valid evidence of Mallory and I having been drugged and poisoned, my argument of being set up fell on deaf ears. I was essentially accused of being on anabolic steroids and placed in a monitored random testing program managed by a company called First Advantage. The actual test was being performed by Quest Laboratories. Apparently, anabolic steroid induced delusional disorder is running rampant in the medical textbooks published by the Ivory Towers; however, in reality, the statistics do not bear this out. Hell, the PDR (Physician's Desk Reference), our compendium of drug facts still asserts that steroids don't enhance athletic abilities. Anyone that has ever watched a football game, whether high school or professional, can plainly see that is not a true statement. There is a reason why athletes use them...they work! They may cause heart attacks, cancer, testicular atrophy, acne, and rage when angered, but delusional disorders, if it occurs, seem rare. Moreover, I wasn't using them!

Chapter 20

The Ghost Revealed

I came away from the second ISC with a slap on the wrist for having done nothing wrong except trying to prevent Mallory from being raped and killed. At my office a UPS truck would deliver a crate full of urine test cups and paperwork with a specific test code written in by hand from First Advantage. I was to call a toll free number at First Advantage every morning to find out if that day would be a test day or not. On a test day, I was to report to a Concentra Medical clinic to give a specimen that would be then delivered to Quest for an analysis. The results would be reported to First Advantage and the Board. Of interest, the results are not reported to the person giving the sample. The board only allows you to see the results in the event there is a positive test. Despite my slap on my wrist "the ghost" was still not happy. I was still practicing medicine, making money and living in San Antonio, which posed a threat to his continuous assault on Mallory and Priscilla. His attempts on my life, and commands to "pack my fucking bags" hadn't scared me out of town. Trying to bankrupt me evidently seemed to be his plan of delaying his incarceration. There would be one more, almost successful attempt on my life, however, during our continuing battle. His other focus became destroying the relationship between Mallory and me. After letting her hear the recording of her screaming at intruders breaking into her condo and getting police involvement, I believe she began getting more difficult for them to control. Without controlling her, there was the risk of her going to the police herself which would be damning to Harry and "the ghost," both. I was finally getting her to see what was really going on and it was scaring the hell out of them.

While most of us were experiencing harassment either through stalking or satellite broadcasts, my parents started getting harassed by other means. After considering sending a letter to Harry's wife, explaining his secret life to her, my parents began receiving phone calls. Harry, scared to death of his wife, knowing anything about KF Higgins and their illegal satellite access, obviously told "the ghost" to play every card available to stop any correspondence with his wife. Kenneth Higgins called my parents several times pretending to be innocent of any harassment toward Mallory and me. He convinced my parents to meet with him and his brother-in-law Chuck Byler, the patriarch of the Byler family, whom I had seen stalking Mallory on many occasions. I also had seen "the ghost" himself walking around Mallory's condo and talking to one of her neighbors. In an attempt to mislead my father, "the ghost" asserted that, "someone else must be stalking John and Mallory...It's got to be a case of mistaken identity." However, it was no mistake that he knew my father's name to pull his phone number out of several pages of "Halls" in the San Antonio White Pages. He added, "I haven't used the Bylers in five years for any investigations and certainly haven't sent them anywhere around Mallory's neighborhood." Chuck Byler described by my father as a "big ole boy," claimed to be in poor health, a recipient of lung transplants. It's a shame that when you sign a donor card you can't specify that your organs not go to a criminal. Anyway, Mr. Byler claimed that "my sons are all in stable marriages and wouldn't be raping anyone and haven't been in Mallory's neighborhood." The two then went on to tell my parents about every letter I had written over the past several years trying to get law enforcement help to combat them. Of course, that was after asserting that they had never heard of me until two months after contacting my parents. As I mentioned earlier, once you are victimized to the extent we've been, controlling your family is almost a given. Most people in a crisis eventually turn to their families and they'll want to eliminate that option for you. In our case they played on my parent's sympathy by portraying the nice, old retired guy and sick, old fat guy that were absolutely innocent of any wrongdoing.

Chuck Byler's youngest son, Jeffery, tried to murder me less than a week after his father spoke to my parents.

One night after leaving Mallory's, as had become my custom, I drove around her complex for a while to see if any of the Byler's vehicles were parked in the vicinity. It was about midnight in the middle of the work week. Certainly too late for any of these model husbands, the Byler's, to be creeping around my girlfriend's condo so far from their homes in Boerne. I parked nearby, sipping my bottled water and watching Mallory's condo as Jeffery Byler circled me in his Ford F-250 pick-up several times, and then disappeared. Fearing the worst, I left my truck and ran to her condo expecting to catch them breaking in. Nothing looked unusual so I returned to my vehicle, finished my water and began my long drive home. At the halfway point between Alamo Heights and Bulverde along Highway 281 there's a fast food burger restaurant. Light-headed, I pulled into the drive thru but couldn't stay awake long enough to order. As I faded in and out of consciousness, the clerk screaming at me through the speaker, I finally managed to complete an order. Most of what I recall about the rest of the drive home is waking up periodically to the sound of gravel clattering in my wheel wells. I apparently drove most of the way home on the shoulders of the two lane country road that leads to my neighborhood. After leaving the restaurant, my next solid memory was coming to consciousness behind the wheel of my truck on a back entrance to my neighborhood. I seldom use that entrance and didn't recognize my surroundings for several minutes. I was able to keep myself awake long enough to find my driveway, stumble up the steps and pass out fully clothed on my bed. The next morning upon my awakening I found my truck had been broken into, several of my digital recorders missing. While their attempt to murder me on the highway failed, they did manage to get away with some of their incriminating recordings. Fortunately, the recording of Mallory screaming at "the ghost" as he entered her condo had already been turned over to the police and wasn't among those taken.

After this latest attempt on my life and, essentially, an admission of guilt to my parents by "the ghost," I compiled all of the facts for the FBI at the national level. I consider these criminals domestic terrorists, as would anyone who has been victimized by them. They fit all the criteria. They're accessing a government weapon that may cause casualties on a large scale, it poses a risk to our financial infrastructure, it can be used for crimes against humanity through psychological torture and control and it allows the criminals a means to impose their will on the public.

Asserting my case as one of domestic terrorism, I sent the FBI a chronology of events detailing both the satellite technology used and the physical stalking and assaults. I included a sworn statement linking Harry and "the ghost" as well as all of the names and addresses of the criminals working for him. The SAPD is currently investigating their "non satellite" based crimes locally; however, I figured it couldn't hurt to clue the FBI in on a group accessing such a dangerous weapon. As I mentioned before, I believe the government agencies would rather turn a blind eye to the criminals hacking into the system than come forward admitting to the public that such technology exists. As more and more people come forward with their tales of victimization, this will get more and more difficult for them to do.

Several organizations now exist giving victims of terrorism using satellite surveillance system a forum to speak out through. I have mentioned two of these organizations. One of them is already working through a legal organization to goad the government into taking notice. As of this writing, a New York State hearing is being scheduled to address the growing frequency of people being victimized by this new breed of terrorists. As for my case, I unfortunately live in the same area as the terrorists so we've been the victims of both physical crime and satellite technology. In San Antonio the criminals accessing the system aren't highly educated "teckkies" or government agents gone astray. They are simply a new breed of sex offender using satellite technology to help commit their crimes.

Chapter 21

No Security

With all of the breaking and entering I've described, you're probably wondering, don't these people have alarm systems? The answer is yes! Don't be fooled into thinking that an alarm system is going to help you catch or learn the identities of intruders. If you are under satellite surveillance they can hear the pass codes you formulate as well as watch you punch them into the keypad. To further complicate things, in my case, the criminals had prior security company experience. They will know their way around your alarm system better than you do. For example, I tried using variable pass codes that changed on a daily basis in order to force the criminals into disabling the system. They did! To keep the siren from alerting my neighbors, they placed a piece of wire connecting the positive and negative leads from the siren at the main box, rendering it inaudible. The system still dialed in, and the sheriff's office still came out only to find no external evidence of breaking and entering. The criminals merely stayed out of site, quietly eluding the deputy walking around the outside of my house. Knowing my pass codes, the criminals actually called my alarm company and changed the telephone numbers it was supposed to be dialing! The only true value in having a monitored security system is the ability to get a written record of when it went off and what action was actually taken. It is a digitally dated and timed record that details the location of the breach; who was called and whether an officer responded to the alarm. ADT was very helpful in providing these records to me and often recorded the badge number of the officer sent out to my home. These records are important because like me, you may not be aware that your alarm system has gone off. One of the deputies that came out to my house to take a burglary report after one of the noticeable intrusions stated that he had been out at least sixteen times for alarm calls.

On many occasions they circumvented my security system by shutting off the electricity at the outdoor circuit breaker box. I tried putting a padlock on it which was promptly cut off during the next break-in. Luckily one of my neighbors noticed my house going dark on several occasions and called either me or the sheriff's department. That seemed to put a stop to shutting the power down! If you're thinking surveillance cameras would possibly help in the scenario, I thought that as well! Two variables have to be hurdled for security cameras to work in this situation. One, unless you have your cameras on a battery backup when the power gets turned off they will not be working. Two, if they are radio frequency cameras electro-magnetic weapons from satellite can screw them up pretty easily giving you distortion only on the recordings. I now have infrared cameras on a battery back-up that are hard wired into a locked digital video recorder (DVR). Along with slide locks on all the exterior doors, this camera system has significantly reduced the frequency of break-ins.

The other weak point at my home, and yours for that matter, is the garage door. Seldom wired into the alarm system, they are easily opened via satellite or a programmable garage door opener that can be purchased at most electronic stores. The satellite trick for opening them uses reverse polarity electro-magnetic energy. With it, they can turn most switches, lights, etc., off and on, even burning your light bulbs out if they wish. At my house, the garage became a point of contingency due to an attic access door that leads to a crawl space into the house, bypassing the door from the garage which is on the alarm system. I eventually locked the garage doors and the attics access with padlocks; an annoyance for me, but worth it to keep the criminals out.

At Mallory's condominium complex the residents voted in hiring a security guard company to patrol the area at night after several vehicles, including my own, were vandalized. An odd choice, I thought, as most burglaries occur during the day when tenants are at work. Even though my vehicle was one of those vandalized, one night, that incidence of late night car vandalism remained an isolated and rare occurrence. Historically, it's been shown that security guards are often part of the criminal problem, not the solution. If you live in an area patrolled by private security guards, don't ever feel your safety is truly in their best interest. A security guard making ten dollars an hour is subject to taking almost any criminal financial incentive to victimize you. That is just the reality of the situation.

In Mallory's neighborhood both the newly hired security guard and the long-time maintenance man were well covered under the financial wing of "the ghost." Whether they were paid or allowed to participate in the many rapes or both still hasn't been discerned. One thing is certain, however; they are both part of it. The maintenance man, a Hispanic male in his thirties, has worked there for several years. Not a resident of the community, he commutes to Villa Tanglewood Condos everyday from another part of town to do basic maintenance on the aging condominiums. He too had been seen creeping around Mallory's place for no legitimate reason. When you think about it, who better to help install surveillance equipment than someone that neighbors wouldn't question being around? He had also gone to great lengths to endear himself to Mallory's parents during their visits to her condo for painting. On the occasion that I tried to show them the evidence that her place had been broken into, they immediately pulled out his cell number wanting to call him to have a look at the damage for an opinion. I thought to myself, "Jesus! Why call him...he's probably helping them break in." Her parents insisted on calling him. However, he never answered his phone and certainly didn't show up while I was there. That answered that question! Even Mallory's parents were surprised that he wouldn't return their call. I, however, was not.

The security guard hired by the management company at her community was yet another fine upstanding member of the community. A former San Antonio Police Officer turned security guard, after being fired from the department for rape. Great! Now my girlfriend, who I know is being drugged and raped, is suppose to be protected by a known rapist working as a security guard. Like the head of the sex crime unit told me earlier, "This is so out there...it's got to be true." The Security guard, a Hispanic male in his forties, would patrol the complex between midnight and dawn with a dog at his side. I witnessed one of the Bylers driving his truck around the area one night. It was a gold Chevy Silverado with a dog crate in the back. Several weeks before the security guard was hired, I had seen one of the Bylers walking a German Shepherd around Mallory's back patio pretending to be security. There was no doubt in my mind that the man hired to do security was already working with "the ghost" and his employees. He would verify my suspicions in short order. I left an anonymous note on his truck politely informing him that my girlfriend was being raped and questioning his involvement with it. The next day he approached me in my vehicle, referring to me by name, angrily telling me he was the only security guard at the complex and my problem was with the imposter I had seen earlier. Of course, that was after he claimed to be a San Antonio Police Officer which I knew he wasn't. When I intentionally questioned him about being on the SAPD, he quickly back peddled into the security guard claim. He then walked his dog past my vehicle and disappeared between some buildings. Ten minutes later Jeffery Byler walked past me in a security guard uniform walking the same dog! It was after that incident I would find out that this same security guard had been fired from the SAPD on rape charges. An officer from SAPD helping us with our case describes him as a "sex freak de jour" and was extremely concerned about his hiring as a security guard at the complex. I reported the incident to the management company at the condominium complex as well as the sex crime unit.

Chapter 22

Gone, Not Forgotten

Whether out of concern or control I'm not certain, but Mallory's parents began attending the Homeowners Association meetings in her absence. As far as I know Mallory had never attended any of their meetings usually held in the early evenings on a weekday. She had told me that after spending much of their time repairing her condo they were attending the meetings despite their not being residents there themselves. After speaking to the management company I was sure the security guard incident would be on the agenda. They were told I had a recording of her condo being broken into while she was there in an apparent drugged state and that rape was suspected. Given the history of the security guard they had hired and his relationship with the Bylers, it needed to be addressed. At first, her parents being present at the meeting sounded like a good idea. I thought it might be a chance to break through their denial and control, giving them a chance to see things more clearly. Control or not, they could certainly see their daughter wasn't the same person she had been whether they believed my accounts or not. By this time she was emotionally labile, drinking heavier than usual and showing signs of physical assault. While her parents did attend the meeting, so did Mallory's neighbors that were working with "the ghost." The security guard topic did come up, but with several of "the ghosts" employees there to direct the conversation away from any wrongdoing on their part. Instead, as Sarah Bocanegra had tried to persuade them before, they left the meeting with the idea that I was having her stalked. Never mind the fact that I had told them about finding her unconscious and possibly raped, they were worried I was invading her privacy! Her parents came away from that meeting lied to, misled and as mind controlled as ever. Instead of getting her a little more safety than me sitting outside her condo all night, the rapists gained a little more privacy to commit their crimes. My presence on the property had kept her from being assaulted on several occasions and they wanted us broken up at any cost.

Sometime after the meeting I had gone to Mallory's only to find her, once again, in a bizarre state. Still conscious, but not making any sense, she kept repeating parts of our conversation again and again. A sign of being drugged with Rohypnol or GHB, her behavior quickly worsened into making animal sounds and complaining of sleepiness. Wanting only to go to sleep, we said our goodbyes and I left to take my position on the curb. Earlier in the evening I had heard footsteps going upstairs to the supposedly vacant condo owned, surprisingly enough, by a private investigator. Upon my leaving, almost simultaneously, the door to the vacant condo slammed shut as I closed Mallory's door. Walking backwards up the steps to my truck, I could see someone peeking out to the vacant condo's blinds. The face looking back at me appeared to be that of my old friend Harry, obviously waiting for the drugs to put her in an amnesic state. The owner of the condo, who was supposedly spending six months in Europe, had mistakenly come to Mallory's door one evening. While I was there he asked us to keep an eye on his condo for him. To further add to his alibi of being away for six months, he placed a note on the mailbox stating he was away and detailing his date of return. Who in their right mind would place a public notice of their absence for six months inviting a burglary? Most people don't even want their newspapers littering their lawn while their away. It's an invitation! We were supposed to think that condo was vacant but old floors aren't very forgiving and their footsteps gave them away on several nights. Nonetheless, I called in a break-in to SAPD as the owner requested, and sent Harry running. Not wanting his wife to find out about his secret life in front of a Magistrate, the push began to break us up once and for all.

Mind control is a very serious and very real technology. When criminals are putting thoughts in your head you become a danger to yourself and to those around you which is exactly the way they want it. The decisions that you appear to be making on your own are really those directed to you and are meant to be self-damaging. At the very least, they're meant to be damaging to someone close to you that actually is the true target. Despite the overwhelming evidence that I presented to Mallory's parents of crimes being committed, they chose to believe I had an overactive imagination and was invading her privacy without warrant.

In a blinding display of mind control, Mallory's parents contacted my parents accusing me of invading her privacy and wanting me out of her life. Mallory, a divorced woman in her 30's and me in my 40's were not teenagers! My father, a retired cop, had heard the recording of one of her assaults and had been harassed by "the ghost" himself. Even he couldn't get through to Mallory's parents! He told them that he had been contacted by "the ghost" and had heard the recording of her screaming at intruders in her condo, suggesting to them that something was going on. Upon suggesting to them that they question Mallory about KF Higgins and Associates, they simply replied; "We don't want anything to do with it" and hung up the phone. Mallory's parents had essentially broken us up, giving way to Harry and "the ghost" unsolicited access to rape their daughter thinking they were doing what was best for her.

Now you can see the danger of mind control technology. The very people she should have been turning to for help were offering her up for sacrifice unknowingly. My father and I could only hope that she would somehow find a way to convey the truth to her parents about the recording.

Threats had become an important part of "the ghost's" arsenal since coming out of anonymity when he contacted my father in person. No longer an unknown spirit, "the ghost" was Kenneth Higgins, an aging ex-FBI agent with a God complex after acquiring illegal access to a government weapon. Likewise, his employee relatives equally think that humanity is their oyster exploiting whomever they please. His terrorist organization is comprised of the most vile and inhuman people to ever set foot in a Methodist Church pretending to be Christians. From the unborn to the elderly, there is no limit or boundary to their terrorism and attacks. While posing as pillars of the community in Boerne, Texas once behind their computers, their language is foul, their attacks severe, and outright physical threats are their latest weapon. Aside from mental control, I knew they were threatening Mallory verbally as well. The audible threats of rape and murder were the first weapons out of the box to try and force me out of the city and leave Mallory unprotected. However, after our last conversation, I realized they were threatening the lives of her parents as well. After pleading with her to go to the police with our story, no matter how crazy it sounded, tears began to well-up in her eyes and their reign on her thoughts seemed to loosen. "I love my parents very much," she said; her voice beginning to crack; "I'll do anything to protect them," she cried. She was letting me know her parent's lives were being threatened without spelling it out, fearing the attack she would get from satellite weapons if she had. "Allowing yourself to be drugged and being raped isn't going to save you or your parents," I told her. "They've already tried to murder us both," I said. By this time, so many men were involved in raping her that it was obvious Harry was hoping someone would kill her in the act. She was having too much recall and he wanted her murdered, just not at his hands.

An interesting phenomenon within satellite harassment is that once the criminals have you hearing what they intend for you to heart they can't stop you from hearing what they may not want you to hear. In addition to the threats and the abuse, one can often hear conversations between the criminals themselves not intended for you to hear. As our relationship fell apart, I had overheard the upcoming plans from Mallory's demise. Apparently, lesser members of their terrorist group were being charged money to join in on the rapes. Obviously men with a mental problem with women capitalized on a chance to brutalize a girl and get away with it. In a broadcast to me Jeffery Byler would sum it up: "We can do things to Mallory that we would like to do to our wives but can't." Any one of their wives would have had them in jail, had they gotten the same results as Mallory had gotten after her gynecological exam. She had bleeding, vaginal tears and a cervical laceration after a brutal sexual attack. Their plan was to send some men over to rape her, telling them she was amnesic when she was really totally conscious. If their plan succeeded, one of the rapists would have no choice but to kill her once they realized she would remember them.

The other plan, formulated by "the ghost," was to threaten her with killing her parents unless she agreed to consent to gang rape on video making it look as if she was a willing participant. Apparently, my having already started police involvement and the risk of her calling the police afterward foiled that plan. The method of murder that they would attempt later involved an overdose on Rohypnol and alcohol for one last rape immediately after we broke up. They had hoped her body would be found several days later and her death ruled a suicide. Fortunately, she is still alive and there is currently a sex-crime unit investigation.

Chapter 23

Erasing Me

Initially their plan appeared to be murdering Mallory and me without it looking like murder. Hence, the frequently occurring drugging, car sabotage, satellite weapon attacks and mind control. I know this sounds like science fiction, but it is happening to us and it's happening to a lot of people worldwide. My story is unique in the fact that we live in same city as the criminals accessing the system. Not satisfied with watching and attacking us with satellite surveillance only, they had to stalk us and attack us physically as well. Remember, satellite surveillance allows the criminals to see you indoors, hear your thoughts, see what you see, and attack you with one weapon or another whenever they wish. There is just about no way of escaping it! Because your brain is the tracking unit, once you're targeted you can be victimized no matter where you go. Sexual assault is the only reason for the addition of non-satellite surveillance equipment to be installed into your home during break-ins. As I have stated before, the criminals accessing this weapon, in my case, and I'm sure in other cases, are thieves and sexual predators using a top secret government weapon to commit their offenses. With any research into the topic at all, you will undoubtedly come across scores of accounts of people who feel they are being experimented on by the government. Not to discredit their misery, but I strongly doubt that is the case. The more likely scenario is that they are being victimized by the criminals based here in San Antonio or others like them. If an alcoholic surgeon and his band of Boerne, Texas inbreeds were able to hack into the system, then one has to assume others have as well. This would account for the vast number of people voicing similar complaints and the assumption that it may be governmental experimentation. The experimentation phase on this type of technology was done long before it ever became included on a surveillance satellite payload. The research I have done in writing this book bears this fact out, with all of the experimentation having been done on consenting volunteers. Government conspiracy sounds much more fanciful but we're really dealing with common criminals using uncommon technology. Obviously, one can see the allure of being able to commit the perfect crime again and again. If someone came to you with the scenario where an attractive woman is being mind controlled, drugged and raped with absolutely no chance of you getting caught...would you take part? In the San Antonio area a group of physicians, security personnel and a former FBI agent succumbed to exactly that temptation with no desire to stop. People ordinarily held in high esteem in our society have reduced themselves to common sex offenders. For years satellite surveillance technology has given them the illusion of invincibility, however, exposing their identities is starting to make them see otherwise. Of course, it's brought me further into their crosshairs.

One would think after destroying the relationship between Mallory and me that the torment would stop for me. After all, they purchased condos around Mallory's and destroyed our relationship to gain unrestricted access to rape the only woman they can totally control. At least it seems that way! More likely, they've spent so many years planting people around her and making their sexual assaults fail-proof that they haven't bothered trying to control another woman; at least, in the San Antonio area. Hopefully, Mallory's cooperation with the police, the many complaints about KF Higgins to the DPS and their revealed identities have lessened the attacks on Mallory. However, Harry and "the ghost" haven't eased up on me, still maintaining the misguided hope that financially destroying me will make me retreat from this battle. Harry should've known better! Every diabolical plan "the ghost" has come up with to silence Mallory and me to date has failed, despite the satellite technology they're using.

He has continued to use the Texas Medical Board as a means to destroy me and outright fear tactics to destroy the lives of those assisting me. While writing this book, a female friend who has asked to remain anonymous, was assisting me with some of the research and most of the typing. Her home began getting broken into midway into my writing as I sort of expected it would. I had warned her of the risk ahead of time and she felt up to the challenge. However, after a second intrusion in which her air conditioning vents were removed, her door locks destroyed and her computer disabled she opted out of this endeavor. Knowing their modus operandi, she was in fear of being drugged or having her pregnant daughter drugged by the intruders more than being physically attacked. She also filed complaints with the DPS and SAPD. Nonetheless, "the ghost" did succeed in scaring off a damn fine assistant but not without bringing some more attention to him. Whether his intent was to prevent the DPS complaint or the book writing is unclear, however he obviously failed at both of those intentions.

Once again, bleach would come into play in their attempts to discredit and revoke my license. Harry and "the ghost," still clinging to the notion of ruining my career, have continued their attempts at drugging me. As you recall, their initial accusations of steroid use landed me in the random testing protocol of the Texas Medical Board. In this absurd protocol you're given a quite extensive list of prohibited substances and instructed to call the Board daily for the order to piss or not to piss. "To piss or not to piss" that is the daily question and please make sure to call before 1:00 p.m. and piss before 3:00 p.m., if you must! The list of prohibited substances encompasses much more than traditional drugs of abuse. It includes: Stimulants, appetite suppressants, medication for ADD, anti-anxiety agents, anti-depressants, antihistamines, anticholinergics, antispasmodics, mind-altering drugs, ephedrine, alcohol, any products containing alcohol, or food containing poppy seeds. One can see how easily you can be set up to fail their random testing protocol. When bleach began to appear in my drinking water and shoes, again I knew what was happening. Despite law enforcement involvement and Mallory being cast out of my life, Harry obviously still felt ruining my career would be his "get out of jail free card." "The ghost" and his employees would comply with Harry's wishes, continuing their break-ins and attempts at drugging me. I try to not eat or drink anything that has spent time in my home without my being there. However, it's easy to forget and no one should have to live like Saddam Hussein in their own home here in the United States. In addition to the drugging attempts, the audio harassment also continued with the criminals hoping to goad me into committing crimes against them. "We've got to get him to do something stupid so we can get him arrested," I would hear several times per day. With the police and the FBI already informed of their identities, I'm not certain why "the ghost" was still so heavily focused on ruining my career. Bleach would have another use, however as I would soon find out!

As I began the random testing program mandated by the Texas Medical Board, bleach once again began to appear soaked into my shoes, socks, and placed into my drinking water. As I pointed out, once someone is on the testing program they're an easy target. The criminals merely have to get an illegal drug into your system knowing eventually you will be asked to test. Bleach mixed with sweat in your socks and shoes creates a smell far worse than normal foot odor. It's unmistakable! If your feet are being attacked by satellite based microwave intended to make you sweat, it's even worse. Heating the soles of the feet to the point of perspiration creates an absorbable surface for whatever drug has been placed in the shoes. For at least one drug, cocaine, it also functions as an indicator of your positivity. Regardless of the route of ingestion of cocaine, once the metabolites are secreted in the sweat and mix with the bleach a color change occurs. The red-orange staining in your socks alerts the criminals that they've succeeded in drugging you. Remember, with satellite surveillance they see what you see and that includes looking at your socks wondering what the hell is going on! It's a dangerous criminal way of performing the bleach test for cocaine that many police departments now use in the field. With cocaine hydrochloride, being an acid, and household bleach being a base, a reaction occurs which creates a red-orange color change. It's not a perfect test but its puts police in the ballpark before moving on to a multiple reagent test for strength and purity. So, with bleach in your system, not only will you sequester the drug making you test positive longer, but your sweat will function as an indicator.

I knew what was coming and prepared for the worse! The Texas Medical Board, knowingly or not, seemed to be playing right along with whatever "the ghost" had planned. At the very least, their refusal to listen to my allegations years earlier makes me hold them partially responsible for what has happened to Mallory and me. God knows they've siphoned off plenty of my time and money that would've been better spent fighting criminals victimizing us instead of the Board. It's difficult to carry all of your personal hygiene products with you all of time and watch what you eat and drink at home. Some things have to remain refrigerated and those items are easily targeted. I began finding needle holes in beer and soft drinks left in my refrigerator and essentially stopped trying to keep milk at home. Several antiperspirant bars that I let slip out of my watch were immediately tampered with, taking on a pinkish hue rather than the normal white color of Sure. Lotions, toothpaste and hair gel are easy targets for tampering so I carry them with me. Anything that you put on your skin or hair and leave there can be used to harm or drug you. In one instance, my toothpaste was contaminated with a fine, ground silica making my gums bleed with each use. Ground silica, found in hobby stores, became a mainstay of their attacks for several reasons including the toothpaste trick. When placed in food, the fine glass particles damage the GI tract causing blood to appear in the stool and vomit. When placed in the air conditioning ducts, the silica coats your clothes and furniture making you light up on infrared cameras like a Christmas ornament. If you have access to some night vision goggles look at a pile of sand through them...you'll see what I mean! Ground silica was found in Priscilla's and Mallory's homes as well. After a break-in at Priscilla's house, during which her safe was destroyed, she entrusted copies of police reports to her mother. In less than a month her mother's home was broken into, her computer tampered with and an entire bag of silica accidentally spilled on her bedroom floor. With no reason to watch her at night, I can only guess their intent was to put it in her food to cause a GI bleed. In her mother's elderly state, a GI bleed would probably prove fatal, so we discarded all of the food in the house. A police report was filed and the silica was taken as evidence. Priscilla's mother lives in Converse, Texas, a township just outside of San Antonio. As far as I know their small police department hasn't figured any of this out yet.

Chapter 24

The Witch-Hunt

My battle with the TMB has continued amidst the array of parlor tricks perpetrated against me using satellite surveillance. The break-ins lessened in frequency after successfully getting police involvement; however, the satellite harassment has not. I'm still harassed twenty four hours a day by the Byler's and their audio broadcasting. Towards the beginning of 2008, the Navy, in a much publicized event, used a missile to shoot down a malfunctioning spy satellite. This happened, coincidentally, approximately two months after I sent a detailed report of the occurrences in San Antonio to the FBI and the National Intelligence Service. The severity of their attacks did significantly lessen after this "malfunctioning" satellite was destroyed. Coincidence, maybe? That is not to say that the attacks stopped. I still get simultaneously threatened and attacked with direct energy weapons daily, but not with the crippling effects that they once had. While writing this book, they seemed to focus on making me too uncomfortable to write, as well as attacking my assistants, as mentioned earlier. These attacks included using microwave energy to elevate my body temperature to distressing levels, ultrasonic energy to continually "pop" or displace my jaw and laser or microwave to burn my genitals. I assure you they didn't want this book to ever be finished for their friends to read who know them only by the façade they portray, not the life they actually lead. Good Christian pillars of the community rarely want their true lives exposed to public scrutiny. After all, the Bylers have spent a lifetime ingraining themselves into the Christian community in Boerne, Texas through their activities within the Methodist Church. Holding leadership positions in the "Walk to Emmaus" and "Vibrant Christian Men's Group," they have tried their best to appear as something they're not. No Christian is immune to hypocrisy; however, most don't come home from Sunday service to help their sons rape and torture people with a government weapon.

In mentioning the parlor tricks of satellite surveillance earlier, I'm referring to the effects of electro-magnetic energy on electronic devices. Almost daily I can stand in my garage as the lights are repeatedly turn off and on while I'm bombarded with verbal assaults. Light bulbs in my house, newly replaced, burn out in a matter of days. While driving I can feel my transmission attempting to shift at inappropriate times as the onboard computer is bombarded with electro-magnetic energy. The result of microwave energy attacks, batteries in all my vehicles rarely last over one year. Battery powered electronics, in particular, are easy prey to directed energy weapons. They can easily be turned on or off via satellite and their batteries severely weakened or destroyed. I can relate two good examples. I have a Grundig short wave receiver in my kitchen that I finally had to remove the batteries from completely after watching them repeatedly turn it on. On another occasion I could feel a nine-volt battery in my pocket burning my leg. After removing it and placing it on a table, it continued to be microwaved to the point of exploding. The effects of directed-energy weapons in electronic devices are worth mentioning because virtually all targeted individuals seem to share in the occurrence of these disturbances. The constant manipulation of appliances that a victim uses in everyday life or attempts to use can be very demoralizing. From the criminal point of view, it is meant to instill a sense of helplessness in the targeted individual. In a sense, letting the victim know that not only has their privacy been invaded, but their ability to carry out their daily living routines can be manipulated. It demonstrates a serious psychiatric malfunction on the part of the criminal, not the victim. Of course, the fact that these criminals are accessing a satellite weapon to control others for their pleasure speaks to this already.

As "the ghost" and his employees retreated from breaking and entering, relying more on satellite harassment to achieve their goals, the Texas Medical Board moved in as their reinforcement. Knowingly or not, the Board seemed to be waiting for "the ghost" to give them adequate reason to take my medical license. In Harry's mind no license means no income and no financial resources to continue the fight for our basic human rights. Several years prior, at my first Board hearing, I had told the panel of Mallory's rape, the attempts on our lives and the obvious attempts at setting me up. They were given police records, a statement from Eco Water detailing the poisoning of my water with bleach and the names of those responsible. Everyone I know could see I was being set up except the self-proclaimed geniuses that sit atop the ivory tower known as the Texas Medical Board. They acted as if they had never heard of a physician being set up before when in actuality, they've been accused of it within their own ranks. A former TMB director resigned amidst allegations of setting up his competitors. Regardless, the Board chose to ignore every shred of evidence presented to them focusing on my situation as a delusional state secondary to anabolic steroid use. Of course, I tested negative for anabolic steroids but that didn't matter to the Board as they answer to no entity other than the state government. Due process does not exist within the TMB and a physician is essentially presumed guilty until there is overwhelming evidence to the contrary. Once their decision is made there is little recourse for the physician regardless of how unfair or absurd it may be. In my case, it was easier to blame me than investigate the real problem. Yet, another psychiatric evaluation was ordered and more anabolic steroid testing. Their testing management company, First Advantage, delivered giant boxes of test kits and triplicate lab requisitions to my office. The requisitions had a test code number hand-written in on them, signifying anabolic steroid testing only. An employee with the compliance office of the TMB verified by phone conversation that I was only being tested for anabolic steroids.

Utter confusion ensued when I appeared at Concentra Medical Clinic for my first mandated anabolic steroid urine test. They had never seen a test code hand-written is on the computer generated requisition form that lists several other testing options.

With nothing to hide, I did my part and provided a urine sample in front of a male witness who finished filling out the necessary paperwork and placed the sample in a Fed Ex bag. Several days later I received an urgent e-mail from Melanie Waters, a representative of First Advantage, asking me to call her as soon as possible! I called her that same day. "You are only supposed to be tested for anabolic steroids," she exclaimed. "Scratch through every other typed-in test on the requisition, only the hand-written test code should be on there," she said. There was a sense of urgency in her voice that told me "I was about to be screwed again." Having almost died from bleach poisoning and watching every pair of shoes I owned get ruined from getting soaked in bleach, I had a pretty good idea what was coming.

Several days later I was paged to my office by Dr. David Kaiser, a chiropractor and partner in my pain management clinic. He was well informed of all of the events going on in my life. He too knew Harry and was aware of his drinking and Hispanic mistress even before we ever worked together. His voice today was solemn and caught me off guard. Usually upbeat and positive this time in a hesitating tone, he asked "Are you ready for this?" "I just received a certified letter from the Board claiming you're positive for cocaine." The urgent e-mail from Melanie Waters made sense to us both now. They had performed the wrong test! The Board ordinarily dragging their feet on most matters they undertake scheduled an emergency hearing for me within a week to suspend my license. Despite earlier pleas for their help against the people whom I had informed then were attempting to set me up, they focused only on the single, inadvertent positive test. Suddenly, anabolic steroids were no longer an issue! At the emergency hearing there was no mention of steroids and I wasn't allowed to mention the years of assault, harassment and rape that had lead to this predicament. The Board, still not wanting to focus on the real problem, took the easy way out by vilifying me publicly. My license was suspended pending further testing, which has all been negative, and a public announcement of the single, unrealistically high positive test was issued by the Board. As of this writing I've also been subject to a board mandated physical exam and neurologic exam, both of which were normal. Several other physicians, including myself, have found that their test results of over 17,000 ng/dl to be unrealistic and especially in that the wrong test was performed in the first place. To date, the only anabolic steroid test that the Board has seen is the one I voluntarily submitted to upon accusation several years ago. I am currently awaiting my hearing to have the suspension lifted. The suspension took place in March 2008 with a hearing to have it lifted in July 2008. However, the Board couldn't convene enough members to hear my case so it was postponed indefinitely. My attorney thinks we may have a hearing in October 2008 if the Board can get it scheduled. In my attorney's words, "The Board does not take into account the financial predicament of the physician in creating its schedule." It took the Board less than a week to suspend my license; it's taken them almost a year to schedule a hearing to get it back! If they're not working with "the ghost," they should be!

Chapter 25

"The Gathering Storm"

In describing events in Europe leading up to WWII Sir Winston Churchill wrote, "Still, if you would not fight for the right when you can easily win without bloodshed, if you will not fight when your victory will be sure and not so costly, you may come to the moment when you will have to fight with all odds against you and only a precarious chance for survival. There may be a worse case; you may have to fight when there is no chance of victory, because it is better to perish than to live as slaves." His comment, at the time, was an attempt to get the U.S. to help in the fight against Nazi tyranny that had engulfed Europe. It still holds true today. Across the nation victims of satellite harassment and mind control technology have seen their pleas to the government for help fall on deaf ears. Unwilling to lift the cloak of secrecy about the extent of satellite technology, it is my opinion that the government merely watches as thousands of innocent Americans have their lives controlled and destroyed by these perpetrators. I consider myself a patriot and understand the necessity of the technology and its veil of secrecy. However, once the system began getting breached by non-government criminals, safeguards should have been instituted to protect the public by locking up those illegally accessing it. This is not due to the lack of attempts by victims who have tried to enlighten the government of these criminals. I have personally provided the names and addresses of these criminals who have been targeting us to the appropriate federal authorities. The Wilson Law Center, located in Cincinnati, Ohio, in their representation of the Freedom From Covert Surveillance and Harassment Organization has been in frequent dialogue with federal officials about this topic. They have even gone as far as to provide members of that group with a letter to present to psychiatrists in the event of accusations of delusional disorders. The letter states that due to the vast number of people nationwide voicing similar complaints of auditory harassment, mind control and direct energy weapon attacks, that dismissing the phenomenon as group paranoia or group delusional disorder does not adequately address the problem. So, the government has definitely been informed of the problem. Their policy of non-intervention is aimed at safeguarding the technology, not the public. In arresting those illegally using the system the door would be open to widespread publicity which would cripple its use in the war on terrorism. However, with the passing of the Patriot Act, I can suggest a different method of handling those illegally using the system.

The Patriot Act provides for warrantless search of individuals that may pose a risk to the United States through their connections with persons aboard. The review of individuals' phone records and wire tapping has been allowed for some time now with respect to those individuals in contact with people in known terrorist "hot-spots." Moreover, in using the term "wire-tapping," I can almost assure you that the government is actually using satellite interception of phone calls and not physical wire-tapping. There are too many people being monitored, with the list growing daily, for physical wire-tapping to be logistically feasible. Nonetheless, the Patriot Act also provides for safeguarding the public from domestic terrorism. By definition "terrorism is the use of bodily harm, threat of bodily harm, or harassment by a group of individuals attempting to impose their will on another group of individuals." The imposition of will may or may not have a political bias. Domestic terrorism is defined similarly with the perpetrators not being affiliated with a foreign power and maintaining U.S. citizenship. Examples of some domestic terrorists include Timothy McVay, the Oklahoma City bomber, and various militant political groups currently under surveillance by the U.S. government. An addition to the definition of terrorism, both foreign and domestic, is the ability to attack or undermine the nation's infrastructure. I would argue that our financial institutions, transportation networks and communications centers are at greater risk form satellite terrorists than physical ground attacks. The criminals accessing our nation's satellite surveillance system fall well within the definition of domestic terrorism, as well as the UN definition of perpetrators of human rights violations. Through their access to the system they can easily defraud financial institutions, use mind controlled technology to destroy people's lives and careers, attack with direct-energy weapons and threaten individuals with auditory harassment to impose their will. Many victims have succumbed to their threats and commands in the hope that the attacks would stop. By using the same weapon against those illegally using it, along with data logs from the system itself, a case of domestic terrorism could be made against the criminals allowing their rendition under the Patriot Act. Thus, with no immediate access to legal representation, the terrorists could be locked away with little or no public fanfare damaging the appropriate use of the technology. This would bring time for the appropriate government agencies to review the data log of the system to make charges of domestic terrorism and human rights abuses successfully stick.

As I've mentioned before, I believe most cases of satellite aggression are being perpetrated by criminals illegally accessing the system. Some cases, however, may be acts of retaliation by rogue members of agencies with legitimate access. One such case is that of Jesus Mendoza Maldonado of Mission, Texas. I have spoken to Mr. Maldonado on several occasions and have received his permission to relate his story in this book. He was influential in denouncing a law school scheme to defraud minorities of their federal loans, diverting the funds to provide law degrees to those affiliated with federal law enforcement and investigative agencies. His role in exposing fraud of federal funds brought him into the crosshairs of those involved in the scheme. He and his family have suffered numerous electronic attacks with radiation and microwave that have been brought to the government's attention through litigation. During the litigation in the case of Maldonado v. the Thomas M. Cooley Law School it was established that "federal agencies are using harmful satellite radiation technology otherwise reserved for National Security and the Military to monitor activity of residences." Part of the federal record included photographic evidence of lesions and swellings on Mr. Maldonado and his children as a result of direct-energy weapons attacks. In his testimonial on Federalsoup.com he wrote, "Without knowing, many are the subject of harmful satellite monitoring and tracking. The power of those using this technology resides in the fact that most who become victims of this assault do not realize it; if they do, they are not likely to be believed and would be unable to stop the aggression." He adds; "For many years directed radiation has been used as a weapon to commit perfect crimes. Directed radiation is silent, invisible and can cause on unsuspecting victims physical harm that can be blamed on natural causes." I bring his case to your attention to illustrate the fact that the government has been made aware of the problem by other people besides me.

Until now most of the legal wrangling involving satellite surveillance at the federal level has revolved around the fourth amendment. The Fourth Amendment of the Constitution provides that: the right of the people to be secure in their persons, houses, papers, and effects against unreasonable searches and seizures, shall not be violated; and no warrants shall issue but upon probable cause, supported by oath or affirmation, and particularly describing the place to be searched, and the persons or things to be seized." The technology currently available to see inside your home via satellite has grown quicker that the Supreme Court's ability to determine its constitutionality. Recent cases brought forward questioning whether use of electronic surveillance constitutes illegal search is included in the cases of Katz v. the United States and Kyllo v. the United States. In defining a reasonable search the courts have upheld that "a reasonable search is deemed reasonable if the technologies used to conduct the search are reasonably available to basic law enforcement agencies." They also include that they are and should be reasonably available to the general public. In the

Harvard Law Review with regards to the surveillance technology being part of a satellite system, it states; "The infrequency of private space travel might be a factor tipping in favor of Fourth Amendment protection. It alludes to given the Court's emphasis on reasonableness of government officials being at a vantage point where any member of the public might plausibly be." Indeed, in Kyllo v. United States the U.S. Supreme Court did hold that the use of sensory technology not in general public use in order to reveal details about the interior of a private home could not otherwise be ascertained without entering the home, constitutes a search. While these cases have involved legitimate agencies misusing satellite technology, questions have also arisen regarding the current satellite technology available on the Web.

Anyone with a computer that's online can access high resolution satellite imaging on several different sites. According to the North Dakota Law Review, in an article about online satellite imagery issues, "Google Earth, which now has 200 million users, started in the intelligence community, as a CIA-backed firm called 'Keyhole' that Google Earth acquired in 2004." The article goes on to address the potential use of satellite imaging by terrorists, online predators, criminals and voyeurs. These issues are not unfounded! In January 2007, terrorists attacked British bases in Basra, Iraq using aerial footage displayed by Google Earth to pinpoint their attacks, according to United Kingdom army intelligence sources. Other issues linked to the recent availability of high resolution, real-time imaging include invasion of privacy concerns and cyber stalking.

According to the Restatement (Second) of Torts, "one's privacy can be invaded in one of the following ways:" 1) unreasonable intrusion upon the seclusion of another, 2) appropriation of the other's name or likeliness, 3) unreasonable publicity given to the other's private life, or 4) publicity that unreasonably places the other in a false light before the public." Intrusion upon one's seclusion is most applicable to satellite surveillance. Cyber stalking, a growing problem is defined by the U.S. Department of Justice as "the use of the internet, e-mail, or other electronic communication devices to stalk another person." Unfortunately, less than half of the states have passed legislation to deal with cyber stalking. California has passed the most-stringent legislation against it, probably due to that state's large number of celebrities within its jurisdiction. New terms that have surfaced to describe cyber stalking include "gang stalking" and "cause stalking." The latter term was coined by Author David Lawson with the same titled book. Mr. Lawson, a private investigator, describes in detail the methods used in observing and harassing targeted individuals by large numbers of stalkers working together. As the court system catches up with the technological advances made in surveillance, maybe those who have fallen victim to this new breed of criminal will finally get restitution.

Chapter 26

Conclusion

While medical research has exhaustively studied the brain, the government has spent much more of its attention and money on the study of the mind. Most people see the two as inseparable entities; however, the capabilities of each are vastly different. The ability to think and reason are tools of the mind supported by the biochemical and bioelectric framework of the physiologic brain. In response to Soviet research in the mind sciences during the Cold War, the CIA and DIA began their own research programs into paranormal activity. In the 1970s and 1980s the CIA, though their affiliation with the Stanford Research Institute (SRI) funneled an excess of forty million dollars into researching remote reading and other psychic phenomenon of interest to our national security. Dr. Russell Targ of SRI pioneered the research into remote reading through Operation Stargate, Operation Scannate, and other code-named operations. For those not familiar with remote reading it is the ability to see, describe and possibly interact at a location without physically traveling to that location. It is a form of telepathy that Dr. Targ and his colleagues were able to successfully reproduce in a series of well controlled studies. A synopsis of his research can be found in his current book titled "Mind Reach; Scientists Look At Psychic Abilities and the Mind Race." Not only was Dr. Targ able to reproduce psychic events in a controlled setting, he was also able to discern, through EEG studies, the area of the brain responsible for its occurrence. Further studies on the area of the brain responsible for the electrical activity that results in thought my have led to the advent of surface EEG processing, the "mind-reading" function of today's satellite surveillance

115

system. Ironically, Dr. Targ retired from Lockheed Martin, a major manufacturer of satellites for the U.S. Government.

In the interest of our national security I have no serious issue with the government having the ability to hear thoughts, see inside a dwelling or attack suspects with directed energy weapons. As it was described to me by an FBI agent, it operates in a narrow window of legal use. "It is a weapon of war for use abroad, according to the agent." My issue lies in the inability of the government to safeguard the public from those illegally accessing the system. In their attempt to maintain a cloak of secrecy over the existing technology, they have allowed a new breed of domestic terrorists to flourish in our country. Thieves, rapists and sadists can now commit the perfect crimes under the protection of satellite surveillance. Because the technology has advanced outside the boundaries of our judicial system, public awareness is currently our only defense. As with other technologic advancements, the government will eventually have to address the issue due to mounting public pressure. Throughout our history the government and our judicial system has always played a form of "catch up" to scientific advancement. The medical industry has seen this first hand in litigation regarding stem-cell research, in-vitro fertilization and chronic life support. As a physician, we are often caught in a gray area between what is ethically correct and judicially ambiguous.

One area where, as a society, we can accept no gray area is mind control technology. Privacy invasion and weapons attacks aside, the advances in mind control technology will have drastic consequences for our society as a whole. People controlled into self-destructive behavior or poor decision making, especially those in leadership positions, will have dire effects on our communities, businesses, and political and religious institutions. We'll never know who is actually making decisions that affect our daily lives, the leaders we've entrusted or the criminals controlling them. As the public becomes aware that the sanctity of thought is no longer private religious institutions will suffer. With our heads hung in prayer we expect God to be on the receiving end, not the government or a private investigator turned criminal. As I've stated before this seems like science fiction but all one has to do is get online with Google Earth. One can easily imagine the technology currently in use by the CIA after selling the rights to the Keyhole satellite system to Google Earth. Albert Einstein made a comment about the advent of nuclear energy that is equally applicable to the advances in satellite technology. He said, "I know not with what weapons WWIII will be fought, but WWIV will be fought with sticks and stones."

Appendix
Survival And Evasion

For the last several decades the Soviet Union has taken the study of mind science much more seriously than the United States. Much of what the United States has come to discover about remote viewing and thought propagation has it foundation in research done in the USRR by Dr. Kholodov and Dr. I. M. Kogan. They were the first to hypothesize that telepathic phenomenon are a combination of quantum physics and Extremely Low Frequency (ELF) electromagnetic propagation. Dr. Kholodov's research has focused on the susceptibility of living systems to the effects of electromagnetic fields and microwave, while Dr. Kogan has emphasized the possibility of ELF wave propagation for information transfer. An important finding in this research was that ELF wave transmission is the wavelength of 300 to 1,000 kilometers is not attenuated by magnetic shielding. Furthermore, the information carrying channel created in this wavelength seems to create a two-way street of information transfer. Thus, a person with remote reading capability can actually transmit information to a remote site as well as receive it. This hypothesis fits well within the Einstein-Podolsky-Rosen paradox a quantum theory that, "no theory of reality compatible with quantum theory can require spatially separated events to be independent." Based upon this hypothesis the Soviet Union focused much of their telepathic research on remote hypnosis and interacting remotely with another person's mind to alter consciousness, mood, or thought processes.

So what does all this have to do with satellite surveillance? These early studies determined: 1) how thought is converted to a measurable electromagnetic response, 2) how and what region

118

of the brain to measure the electromagnetic response of thought, 3) how to artificially recreate telepathic thought propagation to circumvent the need for those with unique ability and 4) how to hear one's thoughts as well as place thoughts in one's head despite any type of magnetic shielding. Decades of mind science research culminated with the technology we now see included on satellite surveillance systems.

Whether you are being criminally victimized or governmentally victimized, there is not much escaping radiation-based satellite imaging. They will see you unless you have access to a lead lined building or a bunker buried at least 300 feet underground. Most people do not have access to either of these so there's little chance of escaping the imaging. Because of the inescapability and radiation exposure of the imagery, I find it far more dangerous than the weapons or the mind control. Almost everyone targeted by satellite imaging reports chronic fatigue, weakness, malaise, and premature aging as a result of chronic long-term radiation exposure. The weapons, although painful, were actually designed to be non-lethal. However, with criminals at the controls of the system, attacking people twenty-four hours a day for years at a time, even non-lethal weapons have proven to cause fatality. Learning to cope with the attacks and documenting any visible damage that occurs is probably one's best defense at the moment. Increasing demands on the government to address the issue of satellite torture will necessitate those with reliable physical evidence of attack to eventually come forward to be heard. However, in the meantime, there may be a way to inflict some pain on your attackers!

Remember, satellite surveillance technology is rooted in quantum physics. Quantum theory provides that spatially separated events cannot exist independently and that information transfers functions in both directions. Whether an information channel is opened by criminals using satellite technology or a person using telepathic ability, the flow of information will function in both directions. Thus, by directing your thought one can actually control the criminals that have opened an information channel on themselves as well as their victim. This will take some practice for those without God-given ability but it is feasible. As I stated in the beginning chapters, EEG processing allows the criminals to see and hear what your mind is seeing and hearing. Visualization techniques and mind alteration techniques can allow one to make the criminals see and hear what you want them to see and hear.

For instance, if you know you're being targeted as evidenced by attacks or auditory harassment, next time you're looking out your window try and visualize Godzilla walking across your backyard. Concentrate and form the mental picture as clear as you can with your eyes open as if you are really seeing Godzilla. Guess what the criminals will be seeing? The CIA loves Godzilla! If you really are under government surveillance this visualization method might even get you a complimentary visit! The same technique can be used to mask conversation you are having with others as well. With some practice you can hold a conversation while simultaneously making yourself hear loud white noise, music or whatever audio masking sound you choose.

These techniques can be taken a step further for those subjected to auditory harassment. If you are hearing the voices of those attacking you being transmitted around your surroundings try and direct your thoughts to the area it sounds like it's coming from. Then mimic the sound, pattern and tone of the voice you are hearing. Remember, this is all done in your mind not aloud. Once you have been able to re-create the voice you are hearing and project it to the perceived source it's originating from, you may proceed in controlling your attacker's words and conversations. After mastering this technique one may be able to control their attackers into seeing and hearing whatever you want them to see or hear. Once you have established a reverse direction of transmission to control your attacker's minds, you may be able to make them feel the same pain that's been inflicted on you. One of the dangers of the two way information transfer channel used in this technology is the ability of targeted individuals to control the moods and behavior of the attackers. In theory, one could actually turn the attackers against themselves creating chaos among those who think they are in control.

Lastly, if you are being physically stalked in conjunction with satellite surveillance there are ways to combat that as well. Do not rely on deadbolts and doorknob locks to safeguard your home from break-ins. Both are easily picked and in most scenarios the stalkers will have criminal locksmiths available to make keys to your home. Use sliding bar locks on all your outside doors so the criminal will have to leave evidence of a break-in when they are required to pry your door open. At least this will afford you the opportunity to get a reliable police report. Also, carry a camera or video recorder in your vehicle. If you feel you're being stalked take a picture of the plate number of their vehicle or the person that's stalking you if possible. If they attack you to get your camera that's even better! It's not illegal to take someone's picture in a public place, and if they attack you that gives you another opportunity for a police report and an identity. These people, as a rule, rely on anonymity and photographing them will get some of them to stop harassing you. Many of them have criminal records already and aren't interested in returning to prison. The satellite surveillance technology gives them a feeling of invincibility that does not apply to physical stalking. Check your state laws on stalking! If they are similar to the laws that California has passed, it may not take much to get your stalkers arrested. Lastly, do not fail to report occurrences to the police. Sure, they are going to think you're crazy at first but as evidence mounts you might actually see some results. In the worst case scenario, if you get murdered at least the police will have a starting point to launch an investigation based on your reports. I have a friend on the San Antonio Police Department that was involved with a case in which a man had repeatedly reported that his girlfriend was being drugged with Rohypnol and raped. He was disregarded as delusional until his girlfriend was found raped and murdered through a Rohypnol overdose. This case is probably the main reason my very similar set of circumstances was taken seriously by the SAPD.

Appendix 2

"Testimonial For The United Nations"
By Jesus Maldonado"

September 22, 2008.

Re: Complaint of Violation of Civil Rights, and Request for Help

From: Mr. Jesus Mendoza Maldonado

To whom it may concern:

My three children and I are the subject of torture by satellite tracking and Organized Stalking as retaliation for denouncing fraud of federal funds, racial discrimination, and judicial corruption. This Complaint points out to specific and concrete evidence on the federal record showing the legitimacy of my claims. Please See Exhibit "1" (attached) which describes some of the physical harm caused on myself and on my children by overexposure to the radiation used by satellite tracking. Exhibit "2" and "3" describe some of the physical harm caused on myself by overexposure to radiation. Exhibit "2" is a Decision of the Social Security Administration finding my electromagnetic sensitivity a severe impairment. Exhibit "3" is a Physician Statement of Disability by the Texas Department of Aging and Disability Services which describes some of the harm caused by the overexposure to radiation.

I was maliciously overexposed to radiation for the first time in 1997, as retaliation for denouncing a fraudulent scheme against the second largest law school in the country, the Thomas M. Cooley Law School located in Lansing, Michigan. At that time I was going on my second year of law school. I found myself on the emergency room with a swollen heart and breathing difficulties a few days after I submitted to the Dean of the law school evidence that the law school engaged in racial discrimination, fraud of federal funds, and the giving away of law degrees to those affiliated to government agencies. At that time, I had been elected President of the Hispanic Law Society and I had been on the Dean's list.

The Electronic Aggression and the Organized Stalking forced me to leave my studies one month away from finishing the semester in the State of Michigan, and I returned to my hometown, Mission, Texas. I left the law school in good moral and academic standing. In my efforts to stop the electronic aggression, I sought help from the federal courts. Although the litigation did not stop the electronic aggression, the following line of cases established on the record the legitimacy of my claims.

A Motion for Summary Judgment established a matter of law the injuries caused on myself by the electronic aggression, my mental stability, and the fact that the law school incited against me a retaliatory federal electronic surveillance and organized stalking for denouncing the fraudulent scheme, including a fraud of student money committed by the president of the law school and former Chief Justice of the Michigan Supreme Court, Thomas E. Brennan, and by the then Judge of the Michigan Court of Appeals, Roman S. Briggs. Jesus Mendoza Maldonado v. The Thomas M. Cooley Law School, et al, W. Dist. MI., Case No. 5 01cv93.

In 2003, I filed a lawsuit against the US Attorney General John Ashcroft to stop the electronic aggression after I saw two of my children with convulsions and seizures while detection equipment was showing high intensities of radiation inside our home. US District Judge Ricardo H. Hinojosa assigned US Magistrate Dorina Ramos to hear the case. Judge Ramos recused herself in light of evidence that Judge Ramos ignored conclusive evidence of fraud of student money committed by Judge Brennan and Judge Gribbs, and ignored evidence of harm caused by the electronic aggression before sending the case against Thomas M. Cooley Law School from McAllen, Texas to Grand Rapids, Michigan. US District Judge Ricardo Hinojosa reassigned the case to Judge Ramos.

On a hearing before US Magistrate Dorina Ramos, my wife testified to the pain and suffering caused on myself and on my children when detection equipment shows high intensities of directed radiation inside our home, and how the readings on the meters go down as soon as I try to video tape the aggression. On a Report and Recommendation to dismiss the case, Judge Ramos altered the testimony of my wife to imply that I am delusional. The Report states that my wife testified that my problems subside as soon as I operate a video camera. Judge Hinojosa declined to consider the judicial misconduct of Judge Ramos and dismissed the case.

During the litigation of this case, the US Attorney General did not oppose evidence of alteration of testimony by Judge Ramos; acknowledged my mental stability; and claimed that the use of ionizing radiation (x-and gamma rays) for surveillance of residences is legal. During the litigation of this case, the US Attorney General did not oppose an Affidavit of a former government agent who was sent to the emergency room with internal bleeding every time he offered to testify in court to my mental stability and to the legitimacy of my claims of electronic aggression. During the litigation of this case, the US Attorney General did not oppose evidence showing that three federal agents (Mark Miller, Michael Rodriguez, and Jeffrey Schrimer, who identified themselves to the principal of the school as FBI agents) engaged in harassment at my work place, a day I attempted to file a criminal complaint against officers of the Thomas M. Cooley Law School. During the litigation of this case, the US Attorney General did not oppose video tape evidence of the pain and suffering caused on myself and on my children while detection equipment indicated an electronic aggression and evidence that federal agencies are using harmful satellite radiation technologies which are otherwise reserved for national security and the military to direct radiation into residences.

Although the Court of Appeals recognized my electrical sensitivity, the harm caused by the electronic aggression, the Court did not address the Magistrate's alteration of testimony to dismiss the case, finding that I had failed to establish a connection between the electronic aggression and the US Attorney General. The US Supreme Court declined to get involved in the case. (Maldonado v. Ashcroft, Case No. M 03-038; US Court of Appeals for the Fifth Circuit Case No. 04-40095; Jesus Mendoza Maldonado v. Alberto R. Gonzales, U.S. Ct. Case No. 04-9908).

I submitted to the City of Mission Police Department videotapes showing high intensities of radiation on detection equipment and the pain and suffering inflicted on my children. The Chief of Police, Lio Longoria, claimed that he was to investigate the case himself. After examination of the videotapes, Jose Gonzales an Investigator for the Police Department concluded that our home had been the subject of an electronic aggression. Another investigator, Ezequiel Navarro, claimed that the local office of the Federal Bureau of Investigation had directed him not to intervene on the case, because of an ongoing investigation of my activities with the Central Intelligence Agency.

Based on these facts, and on the fact established by the litigation against the US Attorney General, I filed a lawsuit in Washington, D.C. The lawsuit sought an Order to Compel the Defendants to cease and desist from using radiation surveillance during any investigation of my activities, and to show cause for the investigation. Without a hearing and without allowing the Defendants to respond, the US District Judge Richard W. Roberts, dismissed the complaint as delusional or fantastic.

On November 21, 2006, Ginsburg, Chief Judge, and Randolph and Tatel, Circuit Judges denied the Petition for Rehearing. The same day, Ginsburg, Chief Justice, and Sentelle, Henderson, Randolph, Rogers, Tatel, Garland, Brown, and Kavanaugh, denied the Petition for Rehearing in Banc.

Judge Kavanaugh, a former White House aide (and possibly a former officer of the Thomas M. Cooley Law School), failed to recuse himself from the case. Judge Kavanaugh is disqualified to hear cases of domestic surveillance because while working as White House aide, Judge Kavanaugh was involved in crafting strategies to conceal from Congress the harmful use of radiation domestic surveillance programs. Judge Kavanaugh has been the subject of a Congressional inquiry to determine if he deceived a congressional committee during confirmation hearings. On June 21, 2007, the US Supreme Court declined to get involved in the case. Jesus Mendoza Maldonado v. Keith Alexander, in his official capacity as Director of the National Security Agency, Michael Hayden, in his official capacity as Director of the Central Intelligence Agency, and George W. Bush in his official capacity as President of the United States of America, US Supreme Court, Case No. 06-9569.

Organized stalking is a copy of the method used by dictatorships to retaliate against those who denounce injustice. Organized stalking includes pervasive street following and high speed road harassment and disruption of daily routines aimed to overload the senses of the target and to cause harm in a way that appears natural, accidental, self inflicted, or the result of a mental problem. Hate groups and groups disguised as neighborhood watch members organize the stalking groups. They fuel support and participation from others by circulating false rumors that the target is mentally insane, child molester, drug dealer, a prostitute, homosexual, spy, terrorist, etc. People from all walks of life from the homeless to professional people, compose these groups. See http://www.multistalkervictims.org/terstalk.htm.

There is no evidence that funding for these activities may come from hate groups, and from federally-funded, faith funds for congregations. Members of these groups are found in the courts, in universities, hospitals, the clergy, and even in law enforcement agencies. The harassment road has resulted in deadly consequences. Dead children have been picked up from the pavement in this area. Evidence that the shootings on campuses and congregations across the country are a reaction to Organized Stalking that includes swift intervention from federal agencies to remove the evidence showing that the culprits were reacting to pervasive harassment.

There have been several attempts to run over my children and me. Some of the identified organizers of Organized Stalking include Michael James Lindquist, a self-proclaimed apostle of a non-Christian federally-funded congregation; Diane K. Smedley, a high school teacher; Ruth Watkins, the wife of a high school teacher; and Christopher T. Lohden, a pilot of a local bank. Without a hearing and despite of defendants' admissions and incriminating evidence, US District Judge Lynn N. Hughes, dismissed the case.

The Defendants did not oppose the appeal. A panel composed of Chief Judge Jones, and King and Dennis found the appeal frivolous and issued a warning of sanctions. Chief Judge Jones was disqualified to hear this case since she had ignored conclusive evidence of fraud on the court by Judge Ramos and Judge Hinojosa to benefit those engaged in fraud of federal funds and retaliation. US Court of Appeals for the Fifth Circuit, Complaints of Judicial Misconduct Nos. 04-05-372-0089 and 90. Maldonado v. Lindquist, et al, US District Court Southern District of Texas, Houston Division, Case No. H-05-97. (US Court of Appeals for the Fifth Circuit Case No. 05-20257).

This case exposes the fact that there are no safeguards in place to impede that the same mentality that tortured and murdered women and children in concentration camps, use silent and invisible technologies to harm people in homes, vehicles, schools, courts, hospitals, and even congregations.

Victims from around the country can testify to the pain and suffering caused by electronic aggressions and Organized Stalking. See http://www.freedomfchs.com/repjimguestltr.pdf .

This type of terrorism could be considered the most serious threat to the American family. Every day we live this torture. Please pray for us. We need your help.

For all the above reasons, I request an investigation of this Complaint and that after an investigation has taken place, to proceed accordingly against those responsible for the criminal acts detailed in this Complaint. If more information or documentation is needed, I will be happy to oblige to the best of my knowledge and belief.

Jesus Mendoza Maldonado

References

Chiappa, K.H. and Ebersole, J.S. 1991. *Harrison's Principles of Internal Medicine.* New York, N.Y.: McGraw-Hill.

Associated Press, "Experts Cite Electro Magnetic Pulse as Terrorist Threat" *Las Vegas Review—Journal,* October 3, 2001.

Churchill, Sir Winston. 1948. *The Gathering Storm.* Bk. 1 ch. 19 p. 348. Boston, MA: Houghton Mifflin.

Craig, Brian. 2007. "Online Satellite and Arial Images; Issues and Analysis." *North Dakota Law Review.* Article 547.

Department of Defense. "Bio-effects of Selected Non-Lethal Weapons;" Addendum to the Non-Lethal Technologies Worldwide Stud. NGIC – 1147 – 101- 98 USAINSCOM.

Flemming, John. July 14, 2001. *The Shocking Menace of Satellite Surveillance*: Pravda, RU.

House Armed Services Committee. *Committee Hearing on Commission to Assess the Threat to the United States from Electro Magnetic Pulse Attack.* July 22, 2004.

Moreno, Jonathan D. 2006. *Mind Wars: Brain Research and National Defense.* New York/Washington D.C.: Dana Press.

Nolan, Keith W. 2000. *Ripcord, Screaming Eagles Under Siege, Viet Nam 1970.* Novato, CA Presidio Press Inc.

Reagan, Ronald. Dec. 4, 1981. Executive Order 12333 United States Intelligence Activities

Schweitzer, Lt. Gen. Robert L. United States Congress Jun 17, 1997. Before the Joint Economic Committee

Simmons, Ric. 2004. "From Katz to Kyllo: A Blueprint For Adopting the Fourth Amendment to Twenty-First Century Technologies." Satellite Surveillance Within U.S. Borders, 650 HI10 St. L.J. 1627.

"Space Preservation Act of 2001" 107th Cong., 1st Sess. H.R. 2977 Introduced by Dennis Kucinich, Thomas Library of Congress.

U.S. Department of Justice, 1999 Report as "Cyberstalking: A New Challenge For Law Enforcement and Industry."

Wood, Margaret, and Alastair Wood. 1990. *Drugs and Anesthesia, Pharmacology For Anesthesiologists.* Baltimore, MD: Williams and Wilkins.

"American Civil Liberties Union Seeks Information About Government Use of Brain Scanners For Interrogations" June 28, 2006

"Group Says fMRI Should Not Be Deployed Until It's Proven Effective"

"American Civil Liberties Calls For Investigation Into Global Surveillance System"

"Concern about Echelon, Global Electronic Communications Surveillance System." April 6, 1999.

President George Bush Executive Order 12333 United States Intelligence Activities. Addendum to Executive Order 12333, July 31, 2008.

Global Security.org, Appendix L., Directed- Energy Weapons

"Mind Reach; Scientists Look at Psychic Abilities" Targ, Russell and Harold Puthoff. 2004. Charlottesville, VA: Hampton Roads Publishing Co.

About the Author

Dr. John Hall graduated from the University of Texas in San Antonio with a Bachelor of Science degree in biology and a minor in philosophy. He attended medical school at the University of North Texas Health Science Center and completed his residency at The Western Reserve Care System in Youngstown, Ohio. He is currently practicing anesthesiology and pain management in Texas. He is a diplomat of the American Board of Anesthesiology and a member of the American Association of Physicians and Surgeons in addition to being active in the Mind Science Foundation, which dedicates itself to the study of human consciousness. This book is a combination of years of research and first-hand experience. As stated in the book, educating the public as to the extent of satellite surveillance is currently our best defense against total loss of privacy and our most basic human rights.

Breinigsville, PA USA
26 January 2011
254153BV00003B/48/P